Beyond the Catechism

Intellectual exercises for questioning Catholics

by

John Moffatt SJ

Beyond the Catechism

© John Moffatt SJ 2006

ISBN: 978-1-84753-054-7

AMDG

Foreword.

We believe in one God, the Father, the Almighty...

If you are comfortable in your faith and your church, then you need read no further than the Creed. If you want to understand the meaning of the sentences of the Creed more deeply, then the Catechism of the Catholic Church explains everything (and more) that you need to know for salvation. You do not need what follows and you should stop reading here.

However, if you are not entirely at ease with your Catholic faith, if there is a gap between the way you think and the words you speak on a Sunday, then read on. The essays that follow are written for you.

Introduction

The essays that follow are a response to a set of problems that arise in presenting Christianity in the modern world, and specifically in presenting Roman Catholic Christianity. The problems lie in the gap between the language of the tradition (for instance the language of the Creed we say on a Sunday) and the language in which we think every other day of the week. In Britain that weekday language carries in it a philosophical tradition of underlying scepticism about the supernatural, as well as assumptions about probability, evidence and reality that have been reinforced by the success of the natural sciences over the last two hundred years. It is no accident, then, that we may find ourselves in difficulties when trying to justify the full range of Catholic beliefs in response to a sophisticated critique conducted in this weekday language, because much of the way we think shares the same assumptions as the critique.

We can deal with this by keeping the Sunday language of our faith in one, hermetically sealed box in our minds, while the rest of our thinking about the world flows around the edges. Yet this cannot be healthy, unless Roman Catholics want to become a sect, relying on the authoritarian transmission of traditional dogmas which gradually become unintelligible and irrelevant to the rest of the world. But 'Catholic' would hardly be an appropriate label for such a group. An alternative, then, is to accept that there is a common language of thought and debate within our culture, and to endeavour to re-express the articles of our faith in that language. If we can do this, our own thoughts will find some peace and we will be able to engage with our world in a language it can begin to understand.

Needless to say, this endeavour entails a risk. For every time faith engages with the reason of a particular era, the expression and understanding of the terms of faith are transformed. But the late leader of the Roman Catholic Church, Pope John Paul II, both affirmed the importance of reason in the articulation and exploration of faith and asked for a continued dialogue with the cultures of our time. Encouraged by this, we can embark on the complex, open-ended, but vitally important task of rethinking what we believe.

Now of course Catholic theologians have engaged in the task of 'rethinking' the faith throughout the 20th Century, but they have often done so against a background of German rather than British philosophical thought. As a result their reflections firstly need a considerable amount of translation and secondly, give the impression of avoiding the naïve but awkward questions posed by the man or woman on the Clapham Omnibus. For this simple south London commuter is likely to want to know whether the things religion talks about really happened and how its claims can possibly be true, against a background of thought that excludes the supernatural on principle and places its faith above all in the conclusions of empirical science. Of course, a series of essays cannot do much to answer the first question: the only real answer there is found in a life of faith. However, we can engage usefully with the second question, which for many people constitutes the principle barrier to that life of faith. This is one of the things I aim to do, using a style of argument from within the British tradition. That will be the main purpose of the first part of these essays.

A second important object of these essays is to gain a renewed understanding of what we mean by 'tradition'. There is a temptation, particularly for Catholics, to think of tradition as a book that has already been written, and that we just need to refer to from time to time. But this misses a major feature of the Christian tradition: its ability to re-imagine and renew itself in different historical and cultural contexts. Intelligent reflection was already present in the Judaism from which Christianity emerges, and remains an essential dimension of both traditions. Christianity was born into a world in which it represented just one world-view competing among others for credibility using the common discourse of the age. Now it finds itself in such a world once more. Its proper, traditional response is to hold the dialogue, to listen, learn and proclaim the Gospel in a language that the world can begin to understand. I hope this aspect of the tradition will become clear through all the essays, but I will pay particular attention to it in the second part.

For some it can appear threatening – if not sacrilegious - to subject long-used sacred language to close scrutiny. Holy things are surely beyond the limited understanding of human beings, and the voice of human reason should know when to be silent. However, I believe that to apply the reason of an era to what we believe most deeply is not to confine our faith within human boundaries, but rather to set it and ourselves free. If John's Gospel is correct, then Christians can have nothing to fear from the search for truth. Where our Christian and our wider beliefs are in harmony, we find ourselves free to commit ourselves more fully to our faith and open to a richer experience of the realities we profess. Reason is the ladder which, in the end, we discard, because the truth we are seeking lies beyond arguments and words, which are bounded by the thought of a people and a time. But the ladder is needed if thinking people of this time are to approach the life-giving truth at all.

Before giving the résumé of the different sections I should add that the argument is not properly academic (for instance, there are no footnotes), is at times tendentious and is certainly not complete. In general I will begin each chapter with a discussion of aspects of the tradition, attempt to see where it raises problems for modern people and then make some suggestions for resolving those problems. I will be referring frequently to the Greek-speaking Jewish world from which Christianity emerged, as well as to authors from throughout the Christian tradition. I have appended a list with a two-line guide to some of the key *Dramatis Personae*.

Parts of the text are difficult. Sometimes this is my fault and sometimes it is simply that the argument is necessarily complicated. However, if this handbook does its work properly, it will stimulate discussion, reflection, perhaps dissent and – at least by negation – engender a family of better arguments in its likeness. Accordingly, if you find some of the proposed ways of thinking helpful, that is good; equally, though, if you disagree with some of them, that is good too. Nothing written here could claim to be a last word. And if you write

7

your refutation you will be helping others who may be struggling to understand and appropriate the faith of their fathers and mothers.

Summary

General Remark

The first part (chapters 1 to 8) is taken up with developing a coherent approach to traditional teachings about God, and specifically the Christian God. Different elements of that approach then provide a framework for the discussions of the second part (Chapters 9 to 14), which reflect on elements of the Christian tradition, primarily from a Roman Catholic perspective.

Chapter 1   Future in the Past and the development of truth

Some different modern options for reflecting on faith. Examples of the ancient dialogue between faith and reason from the Jewish tradition. The ancient world as a model for this dialogue and a model for diversity. Working assumptions about 'developing' truth and speculation beyond the boundaries of experience.

Chapter 2   A History of the Word

Jesus Christ is identified as the divine 'Word' of Jewish tradition. That 'Word' becomes the second person of the Christian Trinity. But what do we mean by 'Word' and how can we continue to mean it in our time? The essay discusses the problem of the limit that the classical concept of 'word' places on the boundlessness of God. It suggests a revised understanding of the 'Word' as the divine imagination rather than the divine reason: whereas 'reason', 'order' and 'plan' imply a limited reality, 'imagination' goes beyond any given boundary to new forms and unlimited possible realities. The idea of form as 'shaping space' will be important in other chapters as well.

Chapter 3   A History of Being and other Big Words

This chapter explores the use of the language of Greek philosophy to develop teachings about the relationship between the Father, the Son and the man, Jesus, in the first six centuries of Christianity. It points out that that language has been superseded in the modern era and sketches possible directions for a restatement of core beliefs: rather than talking of 'being' we should talk of 'energy'. This is, however, work in progress.

Chapter 4   A History of the Soul

This chapter explores the route by which Jews may have integrated ideas from the Hellenistic world into their understanding of the human self and its survival after death. The classical models of the soul available to ancient theologians are contrasted with modern discussions of the self in the mind-brain controversies. The problem of locating the afterlife is highlighted and the essay suggests that existence along a different timeline may be one way to reconcile our present understanding of the likely history of the universe and traditional belief in a new world and the resurrection of the body.

Chapter 5   *Time and Freedom*

An attempt is made to reconcile divine foreknowledge and control of destiny with human freedom, by using different time/causality lines.   In particular, the concept of a time line 'perpendicular' to the entropy timeline of the universe is explored. The chapter suggests how this might make sense of the legend of the Fall, and how it might offer logical space for the concept of life after death.

Chapter 6   *Towards a Natural Theology*

This chapter offers a version of the so-called 'argument from design' for the existence of God. The aim is not to 'prove' by argument that God exists (the author does not believe that this can be done). Rather, the argument shows how belief in God can be credibly integrated with an understanding of the world that includes an acceptance of standard hypotheses of modern science. Key ideas here are the question of what provides a sufficient explanation for certain types of phenomenon, and the anthropic principle of modern physics. A model is also suggested for the relationship between God and the world.

Chapter 7   Evil

This is a discussion of the traditional problem of reconciling the goodness of God with the presence of evil in the world. A number of contemporary variants on the theme are presented against the background of the preceding discussions. The chapter highlights the problem of death as a necessary part of the structure of the world we actually inhabit.

Chapter 8   Knowing and Believing in God

This chapter discusses the traditional problems of evidence and the justification of belief proposed by David Hume and developed in the Anglo-Saxon tradition of philosophy. A minimalist model for the causality of religious experience is suggested, based on the 'empiricist' spirituality of Ignatius of Loyola. A key idea is that God communicates with us via familiar forms and leads us through imagination to unfamiliar ones. Justification of belief in God is compared to justification of the belief that one is loved by another human being.

Chapter 9   Reading the Tradition

The problem of reading and re-interpreting religious texts is discussed, following on from Chapter 8. We return to the sceptical difficulties of believing the improbable, not just because it is improbable, but because we distrust the source of the account. The problem of treating the miracles of the Old and New Testament as parables is discussed. The chapter also deals with history and salvation history, miracles as signs and the development of theology. Rereading bible text and the text of the Roman Catholic tradition.

Chapter 10   Sacraments and Eucharist

Two distinctively Roman Catholic topics are discussed: in the first case, the sacraments and the problems of causality/real effects, as well as the illusion of their homogeneity, conveyed by the use of a single term to refer to seven quite disparate sorts of thing. Questions of sacrifice and real presence in the Eucharist are raised. Finally the gap between the theory and the actual experience of the modern Eucharist is discussed.

Chapter 11   Sacrifice and Salvation

The chapter explores the language of sacrifice and judgment in the search for an understanding of salvation. The 'scapegoat' theory of René Girard is discussed as providing a real structural link between universal human evil, the death of Christ and the ancient practice of sacrifice.

Chapter 12   Ethics and Rules for Christians

A second set of difficulties concerns living the life of the baptised and the problems associated with Christian failure and sin. The clash between the authority-based ethical tradition of the Church and the expectations of a democratic culture is discussed. It is suggested that the primary reference for ethical reality is not a set of commandments, but the person of Jesus, as the embodiment of virtues, in whom the Way becomes desirable. Particular attention is given to 'situational' sin and the need to acknowledge that people can be on a Christian pathway even when they are deemed by the community to be situational sinners. A working model for understanding ethics and Christian ethics is proposed to complement the discussion.

Chapter 13   Reading the Tradition (2)

How the Roman Catholic Church reads salvation history. Re-reading the tradition: a fact and necessity, in which both conservative magisterium and imaginative theologian have a rôle to play. Unity and diversity. Salvation history as non-linear, representing the Kingdom of God in time.

Specific problems in interpreting the New Testament are discussed. The difficulties which arise from the search for historical truth. The place of the New Testament in an evolving Christian tradition. A model for the evolution of the texts and a discussion of the relation between their presentation of the person of Jesus and history. Text as living text and the Resurrection of the Word.

Chapter 1: Future in the Past and the development of truth

In many of the essays that follow, I will refer to the last three centuries of 2nd Temple Judaism and the first few centuries of Christianity. This is not only because most of the key concepts of Christianity were shaped in those centuries, but also because the processes by which they were shaped in relationship with a wider intellectual culture give us a model for the process of intellectual renewal in our own time. Furthermore we can see in those centuries situations in which people acknowledging the same faith demonstrate more than one way of appropriating its core beliefs and more than one way of relating to its distinctive practices. These centuries provide us with a liberating model for unity in diversity among Christians in a complex world.

With this picture of a theology evolving through contact with intellectual and cultural influences from beyond the faith community, we need a working model of how such a process might converge towards truth without undermining the value of what has already been said along the way. This will be taken up in the second part of the chapter.

Part 1: Scripture, reason and the wider world

Whenever people try to start thinking clearly about what they believe, they encounter problems. They find that beliefs which appear to be equally essential to their world-view turn out to be in some way in conflict with one another. This happened from the earliest moments in Christianity, and much of Christian text is taken up with trying to resolve such conflicts of belief. Thus during the first 700 years of our era we can track debates over what exactly we should believe about Jesus Christ, about the Spirit and about God. Traces of this process can be found in the documents of Church Councils, the writings of theologians, and the liturgies and ritual practices of the various Christian Churches.

So much, indeed, is written, that it is comparatively easy to follow the movement from foundational scriptural texts through debate in a common Greek/Roman philosophical language to new ways of talking about the faith. What is not so obvious, however, is the way that scriptural texts themselves – especially the later Jewish writings of the Old Testament and the Jewish Christian writings of the New Testament – have been affected by a similar, though more complex, process of development.

I should like to explain what I mean by first setting out a model of how that process might have worked and then by illustrating it with the example of Jewish beliefs about the soul and the afterlife (a topic that will be discussed in detail in Chapter 4). I do so partly because it will make some of the later chapters easier to follow, but partly because at this point it shows how fundamental the process of reflection, reinterpretation and re-reading is to the tradition from which Christianity emerges. The sacred texts of Christianity, one pillar of the authority on which all Christian reflection rests, are themselves the products of a complex process of reflection by a pre-existing faith

17

community. An idea (afterlife) which is foundational to Christianity may well have emerged in Judaism not through any straightforward revelation, but through a dialogue with the wider culture.

A model of the process

What follows is loosely based on the work of the German scholar, Martin Hengel, who demonstrates the many ways in which Jewish culture, both within and beyond the Jewish territories, interacted with the wider Hellenistic culture in the aftermath of Alexander's conquests. He argues that this interaction leaves its traces in Hebrew writings that have since become accepted as scripture. Now there is no consensus about what exactly happened or what exactly the majority of Jews may have believed at any one time – there is too little direct evidence. There is, however, compelling evidence for a variety of levels of assimilation by Jews to the wider culture of the Greek-speaking world and direct evidence for Jewish engagement with Greek thought in both scriptural and non-scriptural writings of this era. Such writings include the Greek books of Wisdom and Maccabees (1 and 2) and a number of Jewish texts of different genres (tragedy, history, philosophy), some of which I will refer to later on. What is not so clear is whether it is possible to substantiate Hengel's claim of a Greek influence on the Hebrew scriptures that are written inside the Jewish territory during this era (he refers especially to Qohelet (Ecclesiastes) and Ben Sirach (Ecclesiasticus)). I would like to suggest that, in the case of a theology of the afterlife, as found in the book of Daniel, there is at least a plausible supporting argument.

In the two hundred years following the conquests of Alexander (at the end of the 4th Century BCE), the Jews of Jerusalem, Galilee and the Eastern Mediterranean cities lived under Greek rule and were exposed to Hellenistic culture. Many Jews learned Greek, participated in public life and entered into current debates with the rest of the intellectual world. They turned stories from their scriptures into Greek tragedies, they retold their sacred history in the style of the Greek historians and they defended and defined their faith in the language of contemporary philosophy. Two Jewish philosophical writers whose works are preserved are Aristobulus, who followed the philosophy of Aristotle, and Philo of Alexandria, who took Plato for his guide.

At the beginning of the 2nd Century BCE, after over a hundred years of dependency on the Greek ruling families of Egypt and then of Syria, Jerusalem was led by people with a positive attitude to Greek authority and culture, prepared to hellenise their names (the High Priest used the Greek 'Jason' rather than 'Joshua') and apparently even to make their holy city a Greek town, with its own Gymnasium. Unfortunately one of the new dynasty, Antiochus Epiphanes (ruled 175 – 163 BCE), first raided Jerusalem and then, after a number of protests, was persuaded to outlaw the practice of Judaism in its home city. The result was a full-scale rebellion, led by the priestly family of the Maccabees. The Greeks, after some disastrous reverses, gave up the contest. The Maccabees became the new priest-kings in Jerusalem and re-established Jewish ritual and law throughout the region. In the aftermath of the conflict there was a new hostility to all things Greek in the area (from Galilee to Judaea) under Jewish influence. While there were many Jewish communities around the Mediterranean (e.g. at Alexandria in Egypt) whose first language was Greek, in the area governed by the Maccabees the dominant languages were Aramaic and Hebrew.

It is likely that, with time and political compromise and, above all, with the constant traffic between the wider Hellenistic world and the Jewish territory, practical hostility to Greek culture became less significant in all but the religious sphere. From the middle of the 1st Century BCE to the sack of Jerusalem in 70 CE, first the Jewish leaders came under the control of Rome and then, eventually, Jerusalem itself came under direct rule.

This gives us an idea of the cultural context in which any dialogue takes place and any ideas are exchanged. But our particular interest is in the thought of the leading Jewish groups that emerged after the revolt against the Greeks, because it is their thought which shapes the intellectual space for the first generation of Christians. Is there a way of seeing how ideas transmitted through Greek philosophy, that were clearly influential outside Jerusalem and Galilee, might also come to influence the internal debates of the Pharisees, Sadducees and Essenes?

In the range of Jewish writings from this period, we can observe two processes which might have an effect on the theologies of the different schools and groupings. One is internal, directed towards the Jewish community alone, and one external, defending and defining the faith with an eye to its detractors from outside. In the external process, the believer wishes to justify his scriptures before the world. In the internal process, different schools of thought discuss the meaning of those scriptures for faith and life without needing to refer beyond the scriptures themselves.

The Jewish writers Josephus, Philo and Aristobulus all engage in the external process, presenting their faith to the wider world, the first through history and the latter two – significantly for us – through philosophy. Using the tool of allegory developed by Greek philosophers these two are able to reread the scriptures and show that they already contain in metaphor the philosophical truths that are also preached in the pagan schools. However, all three writers wrote in Greek and most probably did their writing outside Judaea, though the young Josephus himself grew up in Jerusalem and fought the Romans in Galilee until his timely surrender. How, then could the dialogue with the wider culture have affected the internal debates in Jerusalem?

Part of the answer is quite simply that there were many Greek-speaking Jews from the Diaspora who came and went and thought and talked in Jerusalem. The Roman citizen, Saul of Tarsus, is an example. But more than this, there is good reason to think that in the earlier period, before the revolt against Antiochus, engagement with Greek thought had already made an impact on Jewish reflection. Two texts from that period, Ecclesiastes (Qohelet) and Ecclesiasticus (Ben Sirach) show signs of such influence – so argues Martin Hengel. In that period, according to the books of Maccabees, just before the revolt, the High Priest, Jason, was negotiating to establish a proper Gymnasium for the young aristocrats of Jerusalem. The fact that he was able to do so indicates a high degree of attraction to things Greek, at least among the ruling elite of Jerusalem. We may reasonably suppose, then, that by the time our religious groups are formed in the 2nd Century, 150 years of contact with the Greek-speaking world has *already* had some effect on Jewish thought among the Greek, Hebrew and Aramaic speakers of Jerusalem.

After the revolt and after the rejection of Hellenism in the Jewish area ruled from Jerusalem, Hebrew was re-established as a common language, and ideas from the Greek world could no longer penetrate directly into internal theological debate in Jerusalem – a debate which would rely above all on the interpretation of Hebrew and Aramaic scripture. But now it was too late to exclude all external influence, because some scriptural interpretations had already been formed in the earlier, open era and some semi-scriptural text was even a product of that era. Yet with their new reading taken for granted, familiar passages could now be used as proof texts in what would seem a completely internal argument for a particular philosophical or theological position. In this way the internal process appears not to need to step outside the bounds of scripture when, in fact, it already has.

Examples of such 'internal', scriptural argument can be found in the New Testament. In Mark 12 the Sadducees prove by a *reductio ad absurdum* (based on Scripture) that resurrection of the dead is impossible. Jesus frames a counter-argument from scripture. His argument works by placing texts from the Hebrew Scriptures side by side: 'he is the God of Abraham, Isaac and Jacob' (Ex. 3, 6), 'he is the God of the living' (perhaps Dt. 5, 23, with an unusual interpretation of the Hebrew), ergo Abraham, Isaac and Jacob are alive. We see a similar use of scripture by the ex-Pharisee Paul. In the letter to the Galatians, he is arguing in a Jewish context, and in order to persuade them to accept that righteousness is found by faith in Christ alone, he has to 'prove' it using the two passages in the Old Testament (from Genesis and from Habakkuk) which juxtapose the terms (Gal. 3). This contrasts with the more 'rational', discursive arguments he uses in a pagan context (for instance the discussion of the resurrection of the body in 1 Corinthians, 15).

We can now turn to some interesting remarks made by Josephus, the historian, about the leading Jewish groups active from the time of the revolt to the destruction of the Temple in 70 CE. In his two works (*A History of the Jewish War* and *The Antiquities of the Jews*) he describes in some detail the teachings and practice of the Pharisees, the Sadducees and the Essenes. He calls them different 'philosophies', but claims specifically that the Pharisees are more like the Stoics while the Sadducees are more akin to the followers of Epicurus. Now it may be that he is just trying to make something foreign intelligible to his Roman audience, but if our picture of how Jewish theology developed is correct, it may be no accident that the claims of the Jewish schools hold echoes of similar claims in the Greek schools. The Pharisees, for instance, believed in a physical afterlife (not unlike the Stoics) while the Sadducees believed that there was no afterlife (like the followers of Epicurus). Furthermore that dispute between them dates from the

23

Greek period and does not appear to have been an issue in Jewish debate before then.

Illustrating the process

Let us in fact look in more detail at this specific example of life after death, and see how it may illustrate the process I have proposed. Notice, first, that from an internal perspective the basic doctrine of the afterlife and a new creation can be justified entirely from scriptural texts like Isaiah's *'I make a new heaven and a new earth'* (Is. 60.17) and *'The land of shadows will give birth'* (Is. 26.19) or Ezekiel's vision of the valley of the dry bones (Ez. 37). Without any reference to outside thought we can develop a theology from them: the present world order will come to an end; God will judge the earth and its people and those who are worthy of life will be given new bodies in the new world, while the souls of the wicked will be discarded.

We find developments of such thought in 'unofficial' Jewish religious texts like the book of Enoch, which was widely read within the Jewish world. In a section probably dating from the 2nd Century BCE it reports a heavenly journey in which the seer visits a mountain in the West with four beautiful hollow caves. In these caves, the souls of the dead are stored ready for the Day of Judgment (1 Enoch 22). At first sight, this development appears purely internal.

But if we look at those prophetic texts from Isaiah and the vision of the dry bones from Ezekiel in context we realise that there was no *necessity* for them to be read as texts about the resurrection of the dead. In context, indeed, they seem better read as metaphors for the rebirth of Israel, as the Jewish people returned from exile in Babylon at the end of the 6th Century. Indeed most of the Old Testament texts show remarkably little interest in an afterlife – a lack of interest reflected in the Wisdom of Ben Sirach (Ecclesiasticus), written at the end of the 3rd Century BCE, and by the position of the conservative Sadducees in the 1st Century CE. The first unambiguous reference to life after death does not appear in Jewish scriptures until Daniel 12, a book almost certainly written at the time of the crisis with Antiochus, after one-and-a-half centuries in a cultural milieu in which life after death, judgment and re-incarnation of one sort or another were common intellectual currency. But from that time on it becomes a significant belief in the doctrines of the Pharisees, who believe in the resurrection of the body, and of the Essenes, who (according to Josephus) only believe in eternal life for the soul.

It is important to acknowledge that Greek thinkers and their disciples very often borrowed ideas – re-incarnation would be one example – themselves. But here we are more interested in the role of Greek culture as one in which ideas are shared, argued over, accepted and rejected, than as one which is the ultimate originator of those ideas. For this is the culture that first allows Jews to debate the interpretation of their tradition in a more analytical manner, against a backdrop of narratives from Persia, Egypt and Greece.

With this in mind, and with all due caution, we can note key points in the Pharisaic doctrine of the afterlife: at the end of time there will be a final judgment, the dead shall be raised in new bodies, while the old world comes to an end (perhaps in fire) and the new heavens and the new earth are established by God for eternity. Beside this we can set the Stoic doctrine: at the end of this era, the universe will be consumed in flames. After that a new universe will emerge and repeat the cycle of history. The soul of each person belongs to the fiery element and returns to its proper place (the heavens) upon death. From there it may be returned to a mortal body in this age, but will certainly receive one in the next cycle of the universe.

It is plausible, I think, to see the resemblances as non-accidental. Josephus was perhaps right in noting echoes between Greek and Jewish schools: Jewish reflection on the afterlife, even in the Jewish heartlands, was stimulated by and evolved through contact with the wider Hellenistic world. The encounter with other cultures has stirred reflection and led to a re-reading of sacred texts; but at the same time, for those who are prepared to explore the wider culture, the encounter offers new and powerful ways of understanding and expressing vital beliefs.

There is one significant lesson for us: reason can *become* revelation.

Diversity in a faith tradition

There is also a lesson to be learnt from this past about the nature of identity and belonging for groups of believers. When Josephus writes for a Roman audience about the Jewish culture and philosophy he calls his own, he is proud to affirm the unity of spirit and practice, and the constancy of its tradition. He exalts the Temple and the High Priest as the unifying focus of the Jewish world. Yet, as we have seen, he readily describes the different groups of Jewish 'philosophies' (Pharisees, Sadducees and Essenes), and even mentions in passing the rival Temple with its own High Priest on the Egyptian border. In all of this, he reveals something of the great diversity of practice and belief that was to be found in the Judaism of the Hellenistic world.

There are intriguing ways in which the Roman Catholic Church has modelled itself in the image and likeness of Temple Judaism. It has created for itself a High Priest, with a Temple (in Rome) and a priestly tribe who have a juridical responsibility for managing the affairs of the people of God. Unlike more word-based forms of Christianity, it defines itself as much by cultic action as by the transmission of doctrine. Its liturgy and architecture deliberately echo and preserve words, actions, themes and physical space from the days of the Temple. A sense of identity is cultivated in relationship to the High Priest (the Pope) and the Holy City (Rome as the New Jerusalem, pace Martin Luther). Like the Second Temple Judaism out of which it came, it exists in a world of many cultures, with which its exponents engage in dialogue from a number of different positions. Like Josephus's Judaism, it presents itself as unitary and united, while the reality - in terms both of depth of allegiance and of practice - is richer and more diverse.

Practically there were many ways of being a Jew in the first century of our era and of relating to the life-giving word of the

27

scriptures. We can use that experience of the ancient faith community from which we spring to interpret our own experience. We need to become aware of the unspoken reality that there is, and always has been, a variety of ways of thinking Catholicism and of being a Roman Catholic. This is not so surprising. God is greater than any human definition, and our definitions cannot determine the boundaries of her salvation and love.

Part 2: The development of doctrine and boundary metaphysics

When faced with the challenge of secular reason, modern Christians have two extreme options for reconciling the conflict between faith and culture. One is to ignore the wider culture and its arguments and cling to 'tradition' – understood here as a set of timelessly valid truths of clear interpretation and clearly defined practices. This path leads to sectarianism and, for thinking people, a sort of schizophrenia. There are (regrettably) signs that some Catholic Christians have a nostalgia for this road, which appears to lead safely back to something like the Church of the 1880s. The other is to accept all the assumptions of the wider culture and abandon all ideas, practices or teachings in one's faith that do not conform to those assumptions. The believer begins a process of demythologisation in the pursuit of a rational version of their faith.

There are two problems with simply accepting the cultural assumptions of any one time. The first is that cultural assumptions change and, most significantly, what counts as 'reasonable' can change.

28

The scientific and philosophical world view of the late 20th Century, for instance, has much more logical space for religious ideas than did that of the late 19th Century, when many theologians were first embarking on a course of 'demythologising' Christianity. Being rational and religious now is different from being rational and religious then. So we cannot accept cultural assumptions about what is reasonable uncritically.

The second problem is that once one sets off on the path of demythologisation, it becomes very hard to tell when to stop. Perhaps, indeed, the most honest solution is to take the process to the limit, like Don Cupitt, who uses ideas from the philosophy of Wittgenstein to justify continuing to practise Christianity (worship, prayer, Christian living) without actually believing in God, redemption or the afterlife in any familiar sense. Insofar as these are realities, they are 'real' only through the practice of Christian life, but beyond that 'form of life' the terms have no reference. Cupitt calls this version of Christianity a 'Christian Buddhism': Christianity without God.

The approach of these essays aims to avoid both extremes and to seek what might be termed a 'critical realist' account of Catholic Christianity. For this I want to make two assumptions which I will set out here.

Two assumptions

The first is that insightful understandings about the world (scientific or otherwise) can be *successfully* expressed in inadequate language and that this is not diminished by that fact that they may later re-expressed in more adequate language. This is important, because I am going to claim that much inherited theological talk is expressed in a philosophical language we no longer use. I am then going to suggest how we might adjust our theological talk in terms of a language we do use. But I will be supposing that, rather than creating a completely new understanding, in so doing, we refine an existing one.

A helpful example can be found in the physics of Democritus and that of Aristotle. Democritus proposed a theory whereby the material world could be explained by the interaction of atoms of different shapes and sizes, colliding with and clinging to each other in an otherwise empty space. Aristotle rejected that idea and preferred to explain the physical interactions of the universe in terms of four basic elements – earth, air, fire and water – which were commutable and continuous with one another. The universe was a continuum and not a vacuum.

Neither was able to carry out observational or experimental science at the level available to us and both were, in important senses, wrong; and yet both, using analogy, provided guiding images for the way the universe is which are still fruitful. Modern physics is founded on the model of interacting particles, while general relativity requires the model of a space-time continuum. Their science was flawed (by our standards), their models were wrong (on our understanding) yet they successfully point towards better models and the flawed first models are preserved in the refined versions.

I want to suggest that something analogous to this process has already taken place within traditional theology, and actually needs to continue taking place. How ideas about God, faith, salvation etc. can be coherently developed in the absence of an experimental science of theology will be discussed in chapters 5 and 13.

The second assumption is that we are allowed to use language and images taken from our experience to talk about things which are strictly beyond our experience. Or that we are, at least, allowed to do this with certain strict reservations. Traditionally such talk about things we cannot observe but whose truth or reality we deduce from things we can observe (like God or goodness) has been labelled metaphysics.

My assumption requires some justification, for although most theology takes metaphysical talk and argument for granted, two of the greatest philosophers of the Enlightenment, David Hume and Immanuel Kant, came up with some very compelling reasons for thinking that all metaphysical talk was fundamentally an illusion. Anyone can spin words and create new ideas by clever argument, but unless those ideas are tied to a reality we can observe, then they are empty of any real content. Theology has been on the back foot ever since.

The high tide of this critical argument was reached in the 1930s, when the English philosopher, A.J. Ayer declared that metaphysical talk was not just empty, but meaningless. Ironically, at the very same time, hard science was discovering in the world of the particle that it could not function without ideas which went way beyond what could

31

be observed and, further, that there were real limits on human powers of observation.

Then Karl Popper, in the same era, undermined the dominant, positivist understanding of science by suggesting that all scientific theory is essentially provisional. No scientific theory, however fruitful, coherent or consistent with observation can be definitively proved. The only guarantee that any given theory about the world can be considered a *scientific* theory in the first instance is that it *could be* proved false. This is, however, a qualification for being a scientific theory, not for being true.

It is the twist which might have disturbed Immanuel Kant that is of greatest importance for rehabilitating theology: that in fact a significant part of modern physics turns out to be speculative. Observation yields theories – for instance that our universe can be described mathematically and that there are certain constants in the equations. But the question arises: why these equations? A theologian might answer 'God chose them'. Someone who does not want to drag God into physics might prefer to say, 'There are an infinite number of universes, with an infinite number of variations – these constants were bound to be in one of them'. Yet, strangely, both of them are engaging in metaphysics, because both are going beyond what can, or could, be observed within the boundaries of our universe.

So I conclude that scientists both do, and are justified in doing, metaphysics, and suggest that, in fairness, theologians should be entitled to do so too, without having to have a bad conscience about it. I would, however, make this proposal: that theologians make use, where they can, of the same metaphysical models that scientists already use to make sense of the boundaries of their observational science. Such boundary metaphysics is obviously fragile, easily undermined by new information or more coherent speculation. It is, however, justifiable and rational. To acknowledge these ideas in theology allows us to enter into a dialogue with some of the most powerful thought in our culture and may help us towards a richer theological narrative of the cosmos. Perhaps, most significantly, it can help us recover the cosmic dimension of our relationship with God, diminished in the positivist centuries.

Chapter 2: A History of the Word

In the beginning was the Word and the Word was with God and the Word was God. Everything that came into being had its being through him.

In the Christian tradition Jesus Christ is identified with the Word of God, present at the beginning of time and the agent by means of whom the universe was created. I want to look a little more deeply at what this language means and where it comes from. I then want to elucidate the problems which that language might raise for believers today, before suggesting some possible routes to resolving those problems.

Origins of the word 'Word' in the Jewish and Christian traditions

At the time when John's Gospel was written, the word 'Word' (Greek 'logos') had a rich collection of meanings and associations. Some of these arose from the Hebrew tradition and some from the Greek tradition that blended with it from three hundred years before the time of Christ in the wake of Alexander's conquests.

In the Hebrew tradition, the Word is the creative and commanding Word of God spoken at the beginning (and God said....) to call the world into being and again (God spoke from the cloud) to speak the commandments of God to his people. It is the word which goes out to the prophets ('the word of the Lord came upon me') shaping their consciousness and giving them the message that must be passed on to the people. It is the written word of the commandments in the Law of Moses, which offer wisdom and a way of life.

The Greek tradition from Heraclitus (C6th BCE), through the Stoics (C4th BCE onwards) speaks of the Word (logos) as a force that shapes the universe and brings order into it. In the writings of Plato and Aristotle (C4th) 'logos' is closely associated with the 'forms', the repeated structures we see in the world around us – human beings, tables, trees, cats, triangles. If the 'form' is the picture of a kind of thing, then the 'logos' is its definition in words. Plato also uses the word 'logos' to refer to the highest faculty of the human soul, which recognises order and pattern in the world and is able to step beyond these to the contemplation of a higher realm of changeless realities. The Latin equivalents of 'logos' in this sense are 'ratio' (reason) and 'intellectus' (intellect).

Jewish reflection on the words of God led to the personification of Wisdom in the book of Proverbs and in the books of Sirach and Wisdom. The two latter books date from the second and first centuries BCE, a period during which Jewish thinkers engaged actively with Greek culture. Wisdom is personified as a woman, who calls people to join her and enjoy her gifts. She is also personified as a spirit, as the craftsman who assists God in the work of creation, and who was there before anything else was made. The 1st century book of Wisdom makes plain that this Wisdom is to be identified with the Law given to Moses as a way of life for God's people.

Without making any judgment about who influenced whom, it is clear that there is a ready overlap for Greek-speaking Jews between the person of Wisdom and the active and world-shaping logos of Heraclitus and the Stoics. John, a Greek-speaking Jew, makes the identification at the beginning of his Gospel. The 'logos' (Word) is an entity distinct from God, at work in creation and shaping creation, and is, like God, divine. Further, this divine being is identified with Jesus of Nazareth, the Word made flesh, who came to teach and save us.

In the past century it has been a common assumption that this movement to make Jesus divine was a very late phenomenon, attributable to the influence of (culturally) Greek Christians. However, it now seems at least as plausible to argue that the identification of Jesus as the human personification of pre-existing Wisdom is a comparatively early, Jewish, phenomenon, which has much to do with the special status of his teachings. For Jewish Christians, Jesus has the authority to offer an authentic interpretation of the Jewish Law, which eventually supersedes that Law, for the wider Christian communities. To justify this position, they must assume that, at the very least, Jesus is closer to the source of Wisdom than Moses.

So because Jesus is the pre-existent Word of God, as well as the Son of Man who suffers, dies and is raised, he is not only the one through whom we are saved; he is also the one through whom the world was made. In later centuries this will cause problems, because Christians are committed to belief in one God and yet the Word they worship is divine. In the C4th CE Arius and Athanasius will argue about whether this Word is truly God or not. In the C5th Cyril and Nestorius will take the argument a step further and quarrel about the relationship between the divine Word and the human Jesus. However, we will leave those debates until the next chapter and concentrate on some of the problems which the word 'logos' itself, in its cosmic sense, may present to modern people.

Mapping the ancient 'Word' onto modern categories of explanation

Some of the concepts encapsulated in the word 'logos' seem helpful in a modern description of the universe. We do see higher order and structure, which we are able to recognise, describe and define and from which we are usefully able to abstract. We find the Stoics using the term 'logos spermatikos' (the seeding word) used to refer to what we would call genetic material. The labelling of material which contains an ordering principle for the generation of new examples of a species as 'logos' seems not so far from the general link sometimes made between biochemistry and information coding in our time.

However, our science has worked with great success from the bottom up and does not willingly cross the border from physics to metaphysics. If there are ordering principles and higher structures, our working assumption, until proved false, will be that these emerge out of lower and more basic principles and structures. We have no need to suppose that they were in some way there from the beginning.

This observation leads on to a more subtle problem, which relates to the question of categories, forms, descriptions and individuals. To explore this, we need to look in slightly more detail at the positions of Plato and Aristotle.

37

The relationship between 'Word', 'Definition', 'Form' and making sense of the world.

For Plato there are fundamental changeless realities, which he calls 'forms' or 'ideas'. These forms are reflected in the second-order realities of the physical world, the world of our sense-experience. The idea of 'tree' exists changelessly, while the trees we see grow and die. The most important higher realities for Plato are ethical: wisdom, justice, self-control, courage and goodness itself. These realities can only be discovered through the mind, by means of its highest function, the 'logos', which is able to abstract from the changeable objects of sense-experience to that which is eternally real.

Plato himself offers many criticisms of this model of two realities and their relationship, but these do not affect the reception of that model by Jews and Christians at various stages of their intellectual histories.

Aristotle accepted the eternity of the forms of the natural kinds (minerals, animals and plants) but for him they were always incarnate in individuals. Aristotle's first interest was biology and he observed in the life-cycle a growth towards maturity (the perfection of the form) and a decline from maturity into senescence and death (loss of form). In the meantime the eternity of the form itself was guaranteed as one individual member of the species reproduced other individuals like itself. Aristotle's God lies outside the changing world, but the forms, as natural kinds, are self-sustaining features of the world, not to be separated from the matter they inform.

Aristotle makes explicit a link constantly made in Plato between the form as appearance (Greek 'eidos' = thing seen or 'morphe' = shape) and form as definition (Greek 'logos' = word). In Aristotle the term 'eidos' is equivalent to a phrase which means literally: 'the what-it-is-to-be-a-thing-like-this'. This is the bridge between the world of the senses (how things appear) and the world of abstraction in deliberation, understanding, explanation, logic. But it is in the gap between the sharpness of verbal definition and the indefinite variety of examples of any defined kind that the problems will arise.

For Jews and Christians, Aristotle's picture of the world of natural kinds dovetails neatly with the account of creation in Genesis 1. Animals and plants are established once and for all 'in their kinds'. We can then borrow freely from Plato and the Stoics (if we want to) and identify an ordering principle (logos) which both contains the archetypes of the kinds and establishes material examples of them in the universe. This same 'logos' contains both the commands which order the processes of the universe and those which govern human behaviour. Christianity identifies this Word as a person, as we have seen in the Gospel of John and can see in the narratives of the transfiguration, while Rabbinic Judaism will give it its apotheosis in the Zohar, the transcendent Glory from which the written Torah (Law) emerges.

'Logos' as blueprint and 'logos' as the mind of the architect - the problems of clear definition in the natural and divine order.

There is a close relation between 'logos' as divine mind and 'logos' as definition. The universe has an architect and is constructed according to a blueprint. The blueprint pre-exists in the mind of the architect and is instantiated in the architect's creation. But for this model to work, form as appearance must be commutable with form as definition. The final structure is designed according to a clear plan.

Unfortunately such a 'logos' is too small, not just for God, who is always greater, but for our world as well. Since Darwin, we can no longer think of the natural kinds as eternal. They have evolved through time and can continue to evolve. Even within the boundaries of an existing form, there are many variations, but, as we now understand it, the boundaries of the form themselves are also open to variation. When some variations are discarded on a given evolutionary trajectory, new possibilities for variation are opened up. The model of the cosmic blueprint with its closed endpoint and sharp lines of definition seems contradicted by the rich variety, variability and particularity of the things that are. We must ask not just if every detail of every form (down to hair and nails) is eternally embedded in the blueprint, but if every detail of every phase of evolutionary development of every temporary form is in some way embedded in the mind of God. The 'logos' as 'definition' seems scarcely equal to the challenge.

Worse still, such fluidity of form and structure is not just found in the realm of biology. The very categories and concepts which we use to explain and make sense of our existence and to structure our common life can also shift and change. In their different ways the philosophers Hegel, Marx, and Wittgenstein, together with the psychologist, Freud, have forced us to think in new ways about our thinking. We can no longer be uncritical about the way we happen to see, judge and explain the world and our experience of it. The way we reason – the way I am now reasoning – is the product of a culture, a psychology, a way of life. My argument is part of a language game, and though some language games are more equal than others, none can establish its primacy beyond dispute. The interpreting word has boundaries as fluid as the forms it attempts to describe.

But if the categories with which we see and judge the world are subject to change and evolution, why should we suppose a divine 'logos', whose categories are distinct and changeless, when there is no sure base for this analogy in human experience? For any two given categories which are close together, we can suppose a third: given a table with three legs and a table with four legs we can suppose a table with five legs. Must all of these pre-exist in the divine Word?

Rethinking the Word

Perhaps we need to rethink the Word. And here I would suggest two strategies. The first is to loosen the traditional connection between form and definition. Instead of seeing a given form as equivalent to a sharply defined concept, we should think of it rather as a label for an inner logical space, bounded by parameters, but which can be filled in a (perhaps endless) variety of ways. That is not as difficult as it sounds, and I will illustrate what I mean here in the next paragraph. The second strategy I propose is to identify the 'logos' not so much with the recognising/knowing function of the mind but rather with the imagination, which, given one shape, sees the possibility of others – sees the outer logical space implied by any given form.

So let me illustrate by an example. The term hexagon has an inner logical space dependent on its definition. An infinite variety of hexagons can occupy that logical space, varying in size and in internal angles. However, 'hexagon' also has an outer logical space equally implied by its definition. This outer space is the implied possibility of other two-dimensional polygons. In this space the imagination has room to discover octagons and dodecagons and other geometrical figures. But then again 'two-dimensional polygon' itself sets parameters of a further inner and outer logical space which lead the imagination to explore three and multi-dimensional figures.

In principle, any given form implies every possible variety of instantiation, whether we know them or not and whether they are all realised or not. Equally any given form implies related variant forms in an outer logical space. The form 'horse' implies colts of many colours, shapes and sizes in the inner logical space, but implies zebras, mules, donkeys (and unicorns) in the immediate outer logical space surrounding the form. So the world of forms has a similar status to the world of numbers: the totality is already implied, but for the human

42

mind, the implications wait to be discovered and discovery comes through an exercise of the imagination.

But if our newly conceived 'logos' is to be truly divine, then it cannot be limited to being a template for our particular and limited universe. As the divine imagination it is the space which contains all possibility of all possible logical spaces under which things can exist in all possible worlds. The human imagination can only make a finite voyage of discovery into these spaces. In the divine imagination their infinity is present.

Translating the 'Word as imagination' into the second person of the Christian Trinity.

How might such an imagination relate to our universe?

The Word is the divine imagination, the space containing all logical spaces, each of which has its own inner shape. The inner logic of each space is like a gravitational field, placing limits on the pathways that can be taken within that space. The space is a womb in which a reality can grow and take its individual shape.

God chooses space for our world, which grows freely within the boundaries of its womb, 'choosing' from the pathways that the shape of its space implies. In this way the world becomes one instance of the infinite possibilities constituting the imagination of God.

But this leaves us a long way from the second person of the Christian Trinity. It is hard to turn such an abstract faculty of God into a person in anything like our colloquial sense of the word. It is perhaps more difficult for us, who think of 'person' in more affective terms, than for the ancients. It is one thing to find a formula which captures the logical aspect of the relationship between God, Word and world, but we must acknowledge that this is, on its own, incomplete without the higher things which are important to us as human beings: a self-consciousness experienced in relationship with others, the categories of love and of goodness. We need to find in God the transhuman and eternal guarantee that what makes human life worth living is indeed ultimate.

A first step is to see that we have space for the relationship of love. We could use as analogies the artist and her work or the mother and her child. The world selected by God is the object of love and is loveable. It is also good. These are the ultimate parameters of the space shaped by the divine imagination. In love, then, the Word wills the world gestating within it, called into being by the Father. As intelligent and free subjects emerge within that world, their selves grow in a social space shaped by justice, integrity, courage, honesty, self-control, wisdom. They find themselves called into the transhuman love whose echoes they experience in their human lives.

Chapter 3:   A History of Being and other Big Words.

'True God from true God, begotten, not made, of one being with the Father....' *(Council of Nicea, 1ˢᵗ Council of Constantinople 381)*

'Of one being with the Father, according to the divinity, and of one being with us according to the humanity...the characteristic of each nature being preserved and meeting in one person and one hypostasis'

(Council of Chalcedon 451)

These are quotations from foundational documents in Christianity. They are part of the reason why we worship God as Father, Son and Spirit, and part of the reason why we worship Jesus as true God and true man. They represent an attempt by Christians of the 4ᵗʰ and 5ᵗʰ Centuries to articulate their beliefs about God, Jesus and the Spirit in the language of their time.

We can note some crucial technical terms. 'Being' is important in both quotations. God is the 'one who is' and the Son is 'of one being with the Father'. In the quotation from Chalcedon, we see a second technical term, 'hypostasis', which can be translated variously as 'person', 'substrate', 'reality' or 'subject'. The term was initially used by Christians to refer to each of the three persons of the Trinity in the one God. Here, it becomes central in the explanation of the relationship between the second person of the Trinity (the Son) and the human being, Jesus of Nazareth. The formula for this runs 'two natures (or

45

'beings') in one hypostasis (reality)'. 'Nature' itself provides us with a third technical term.

I want to look at just these two cases: the formula from the Creed, describing the Son as 'of one being with the Father' and the formula from the council of Chalcedon, describing the union of the Son of the God and the Son of Man as 'two natures in one reality'. I want to sketch how these items of faith came to be expressed in the scientific/philosophical language of an era, in language largely shaped by Aristotle. In the process we will see, however, that the Christian uses are an extension of that common language, expanding the terms beyond the reach of their analogical base in human experience. I should then like to spell out (as before) the ways in which the philosophical/scientific language of the formulae has been superseded in the last three hundred years and suggest some ways towards restating them in the philosophical/scientific language of our own time.

We begin with the background to the language of those ancient formulations.

The language of being and Greek philosophy-science: reductive and multi-level explanation.

Much of Greek philosophy is taken up with explaining natural phenomena – meaning, quite precisely, things as they appear to us. Some of the explanations are reductive in style. They seek to explain higher-order, complex phenomena in terms of lower-order, simple phenomena. Thales (C7th BCE) explains the origins of things in terms of water, Heraclitus takes fire to be the basic element which explains everything there is.

Aristotle's explanations, in contrast, accept that higher-order and lower-order phenomena are equally real. Thus, when explaining a complex phenomenon or event, it will sometimes be necessary to explain in terms of the whole – the sort of thing being investigated – and sometimes in terms of its constituents – what makes up the thing being investigated. When we view things from the point of view of what they are as a whole, we are looking at their 'form'. When we view things from the point of view of their constituents, we are looking at their 'matter'.

A bear can be considered as a large hairy animal with claws and sharp teeth, which lives in the wild and occasionally eats human beings (its form) or from the point of view of its interior organs, body tissue and humours (its matter). When seeking an explanation, we will look for an explanation sometimes at the level of form, sometimes at the level of the material. So, why did the bear eat the philosopher? Because bears are predatory carnivores, this bear happened to be hungry and the philosopher chose the wrong cave to escape illusion from. Why was the bear hungry? Because he had not ingested food recently and because the imbalance of hot and cold, moist and solid within him caused the urge to look for food. The two different levels of explanation, formal and material, are appropriate to the different questions. Why is the statue holding a trident? Because it is a statue of Poseidon and Poseidon has a trident. Why is the statue green? Because the bronze of which it is made has been exposed to the elements too long.

The labels 'form' and 'matter' are relative. Blood, which is a constituent of the bear, can be broken down into its own (Aristotelian) constituents of the hot and the moist – and these constituents are then used to explain some of the characteristics of blood. The terms are closely tied to a model of observational science which catalogues realities according to their appearance and the sorts of thing they do.

When it comes to talking about 'being', Aristotle partly catalogues, partly refines standard usage. This usage is often closely tied to the grammar and colloquialisms of ancient Greek, which do not transfer easily to all other languages. We will only look here at some of the uses of 'being' which are of immediate concern to us.

Sometimes by 'being', we mean a complete thing, matter in a particular form: a bear, or this bear in particular. Sometimes we are referring specifically to the form: bears in general, what it is to be a bear, the nature of bears. This meaning of 'being' is then equivalent to the terms 'form', 'nature', 'what it is to be an x' and the Latin term 'essence'. And this is where there is a crossover between form as *appearance* (what you see) and form as *definition* (what you say): the diagram of the bear is equivalent to its verbal description.

Sometimes 'being' can refer to the collection of matter that constitutes this particular individual. For 'being' in this sense, Aristotle sometimes uses a term which can be rendered 'substrate'; at others he uses the phrase 'a this-thing-here' (a particular thing). It is to capture this concept that the Stoics coined the term 'hypostasis'.

Aristotle's science is highly descriptive; it is closely tied to the categories in which we already see and talk about the world. The form – matter relationship, which holds for things-out-there, is therefore not accidentally a mirror of our descriptive language of subject and predicate. The subject is the individual (the hypostasis) which we identify as there, before we say anything about it. The 'form'/'nature' is the primary predicate. This (hypostasis) is a bear (form/nature). More usually we refer to the individual via the 'form', because we usually recognise an individual instantly as a particular sort of thing: The bear is hungry (this individual, which is a bear, is hungry).

This connection between the language of hypostasis and being and the way we use language to describe our world is important in the later Christian debates. But it is equally important to see that the language arises out of an interpretation of experience in which form is seen 'incarnate' in matter and in which matter individuates or instantiates form, providing us with particular examples of different sorts of thing.

The language of 'being' in classical Christian discussions about the Trinity

We are now in a position to see more clearly what is meant by 'of one being with the Father'. This is not, in the first instance, a statement claiming that the Son and the Father are both a part of one thing – they have separate identities. It is, rather, a statement that they share the same nature: both these individuals are God, as what follows in the Creed makes clear ('God from God'). To be God is to be a sort of thing as well, and the Creed is claiming that the individual Son or Word shares the divine attributes and activities of the Father.

The argument over this formulation was not settled at the Council of Nicea at which it was proposed in 325 CE. In fact it rumbled on until the Council of Constantinople at the end of the fourth century. The background work of three Christian theologians from Cappadocia (in modern Turkey) was particularly important – alongside political exigencies – in developing the Creed of 381 which we use today. Basil, Gregory of Nyssa and Gregory Nazianzen moved the debate on by developing the language of the Trinity using the term 'hypostasis'. They argued that Father, Son and Spirit are three hypostases (individuals), which share the one being 'God'. Just as many people can share the one attribute 'human-being' and there is only one humanity, so too the three persons of the Trinity share the one attribute 'God' and there is only one deity.

At this point we need to ask how this squares with belief in one God – which surely implies only one individual (doesn't it?). Surely, if you have three individuals, all of whom are God, then you have three Gods? The three theologians from Cappadocia were united in their sensitivity to this problem. The examples that follow paraphrase some of the responses with which they met the accusation of believing in three Gods.

1.   Accept that we cannot know anything about the being of God, but that what we can do is point to the unity of his activity. So, we define the oneness of God from the unity of God's activity

as it appears to us, without speculating about structures within the Trinity.

2.   Alternatively, we might try and seek to establish the unity of God by speaking of the unique set of relationships within God.

3.   Or we can say that the being/nature of God is different from being/nature as experienced by us. We are familiar with there being many instances of particular forms, but God is different, only being instantiated in three individuals.

Nearly nine hundred years later, Thomas Aquinas, who was reformulating Theology in the language of Aristotle, ingeniously solved the problem by arguing that a non-material form (God is, after all a spiritual being) is its own instance; thus 'God' is both the form of each hypostasis of the Trinity and the individuating principle which makes them all one – a sort of hypo-hypostasis.

But notice: each solution to the problems raised by using the language of 'being' and 'hypostasis' detaches the terms we are using to 'explain' God from their base in our experience. And if we want to understand how the words are being used and what they mean, we can only explain by referring to the conflicting statements which they are attempting to reconcile. Language is being pushed to its limit and the relationship between the terms which are to be explained and the terms which are supposed to be doing the explaining becomes circular.

Shifts in the use of language with the debate over Jesus, God and Man (5th Century CE).

A similar process can be observed in the debate over the relationship between the divine Word and the person Jesus. The two principal protagonists are Cyril of Alexandria and Nestorius of Antioch. The school of Antioch was interested in close reading of the sacred texts and generated its theological statements in close harmony with the language of scripture, while the school of Alexandria, making free use of the allegorical method, more easily developed a theology independent of the text that was shaped by the need for coherence with the philosophy of the age.

In the 5th Century, Nestorius proposed a model, rooted in scripture and based on an image: the divine being dwells in the human being as in a temple. This picture raises no particular philosophical problems: the two beings co-exist side by side, each with their own nature and each with their own individuating substrate, but they are in a unique relationship with each other. In some way the Word shares the experience of the man, although it does not suffer and die in the strict sense of the words – but then the Word, as God, cannot suffer and die.

Cyril objected that the Son must indeed suffer, die and rise, because that is what the scripture says. To deny that the Word suffers is to deny that the incarnation proclaimed in the Creed is real. If the Word and the man have separate hypostases, then they have separate experiences, and what is said of the one cannot be said of the other.

Accordingly there must be one hypostasis after the incarnation and, correspondingly, one new nature that combined being human with being divine. Again, Cyril's position is consistent with normal use of the language of nature and hypostasis.

However, this position is rejected because it implies a change in the nature of the divine Word, and God cannot change. A compromise is adopted. There is one hypostasis (the Word) for the divine nature of the Word and the human nature of Jesus. The two natures coexist in the one hypostasis without separation and without confusion. What is said of the Word (the Word is eternal) is true of the man and what is said of the man (Jesus died and rose again) is true of the Word in virtue not of their natures but of the shared hypostasis. The distinction is spelt out further two hundred years later, in the 7th Century by the statement that each nature has a separate will and a separate activity, which are nevertheless in perfect harmony.

Once again, though, the words have been cut off from their roots in our experience. In terms of image, there is no practical difference between the final, 7th Century model and the temple image of Nestorius. The crucial theoretical difference is the use of the words 'one hypostasis'. But note, we have not really discovered a surprising new fact in philosophy-science, that one hypostasis (at least in this case) can have two natures. Rather we have come up with a formula using familiar language in an unfamiliar sense that can only be understood in terms of the contradictions it seeks to reconcile.

The categories of human thought, based as they are on human experience, can only provide analogies for divine realities, which are, by definition, beyond what we are capable of experiencing. Pushed to their limit they break down. Yet we need to make the attempt to find some harmony between what our faith asks us to believe and the way we practically think about and make sense of the world at large. The problem for us in the language so far discussed is not so much that it breaks down as that it is irrelevant. This is simply not how we begin to talk about reality now.

The direct descendant of Aristotelian form, 'species', continues to be useful when talking about natural kinds in biology, which is still influenced by Aristotle's system of classification. Again, molecular biology highlights the relationship genotype (DNA) – phenotype (physical entity), capturing something of the old matter-form relationship. The difference, however, is that for Aristotle the form could be validly used to provide the primary explanation for a phenomenon, while the phenotype-genotype relationship favours reductive explanation: the phenotype is the expression of the evolved genotype in the context of its environment. Form is thus *derivative* from matter and so matter will always provide the primary explanation.

Furthermore, as we have already seen, thanks to Darwin and biochemistry, it is no longer as easy to think of forms as eternal incarnate (or indeed discarnate) realities, because the forms themselves (the phenotypes) change as the genotypes mutate. Matter is primary

54

and form is secondary, at least as far as experimental science is concerned.

Mapping 'form' onto 'information'.

The theoretical equivalent of 'form' in modern scientific/philosophical discussion is probably 'information'. Like the 'form' of Aristotle it is a general term that links our use of language with material structures, artificial and natural, from the simplest communication provided by a ray of light to the complex encoded instructions of DNA and their expression in a living creature. The use of the term makes no assumptions about the priority of information – information evolves in complexity with the universe. But it is practically possible to represent the same information in a number of different material instantiations, whether by cloning a sheep, or by turning a visual image into a digital code, or a record into a CD. It seems then, that information can exist without being dependent on any one material expression of itself. This is not too far from what Aristotle might have claimed for his forms.

Hypostasis as 'entity' - a useful label, but not a scientific term

'Hypostasis' might be rendered 'underlying structure', 'reality' or 'entity' but these are only labels by which we conveniently refer to a specific material structure – perhaps a complex organic molecule, perhaps a proton, perhaps a quark. The label would, however, have nothing to do with the explanation. The explanation comes from examining the specific properties of that molecule, of that proton, of that quark in its environment. The specific label 'proton' points us towards explanations. The general label 'entity' tells us nothing – it is scientifically useless.

'Being' and the categories of modern science

'Being' is also a term which is too general to be of use. For Aristotle, working within the grammatical tricks of the Greek language, its generality meant that it was the property which every existent thing possessed. For many of us, however, it is not a property at all, at least not in the sense of a defining quality (Kant, Quine). More significantly it does not feature in our scientific explanations of the physical world. Our explanations of the universe use the laws of motion modified by Einstein and by Quantum Theory. They refer to the constants of nature discovered by theory and experiment, and deal with energy as the ultimate reality, from which the different forms of matter are derived. Where there is energy, there are things. Where energy is structured, there is information.

Translating ancient doctrines

The process of arguing towards the Trinity and of arguing towards the hypostatic union was important for the Church because the formulae that were produced encapsulated the apparently contradictory things Christians wanted to hold true, on the basis of their reading of scripture and the tradition and on the basis of their experience in prayer and liturgy. We want God to be one, but we also want the Son of God and the Spirit to be equally divine and eternal with the Father. We want Jesus to be true God and true man, but we want him to be one subject of all that the Gospel says of him. That is our evolved belief, which we accept as true, because we trust in the work of the Spirit, who can communicate truth through incomplete and inadequate arguments. This trust, however, should not distract us from an obligation to restate the truths we believe, with the help of the same Spirit, in fuller and more adequate terms, for our own good, and for the good of those who do not yet believe.

Here are some suggestions as to how the work of translation might begin.

If energy is the fundamental reality in the universe, then God is the ultimate source of that energy. If the movement and transformation of energy is structured according to particular laws and constants, then those structures, and the structures into which the universe evolves, through which the energy of the universe flows, are set in place by God. If the universe creates information in dependence on God, then there are analogues of that information in God. If God interacts with the universe, then she does so through an energy transfer, which costs her no energy. If to be there is to be energy, then God is energy structured in a way we cannot understand, inexhaustible in a way we cannot understand, non-material in a way we cannot understand, personal in a

57

way we cannot understand. But although we do not understand, we may at least be able to refine the boundaries of our non-understanding.

For the three individuals in the one God, each bearing the property 'God', we have to take a step back from the strong position of the Cappadocians and go back to analogies, perhaps supplementing traditional analogies (the fountain, stream and sea of Tertullian, the memory, understanding and will of Augustine). We want to answer the question, how can three individuals make one entity without losing their identity? What does it mean for one individual to generate two others timelessly and for the three together to be one super-individual?

A water molecule provides an incomplete analogy. The characteristics of the water molecule are the product of the characteristics of the hydrogen and oxygen molecules which make it up. The analogy is incomplete because it does not allow us to say that the hydrogen atom has the properties of water or that the oxygen atom has the properties of water. Nevertheless, it gives a picture of a relationship between different forms of structured energy which preserves the distinctness of the individuals at the same time as producing a unified effect – the unity of a system.

A vision of Ignatius of Loyola provides the musical image of a triad. One individual chord is created by the relationship of the three notes. It does not capture the relationship of 'generation' between Father and Son or 'proceeding' between Father and Spirit, which traditional theology derives from scripture, but it does give a model for a reality which consists in its relationships. One could naturally supplement this with the image of a complex wave, which 'carries' energy and is the sum of three simple waves.

To capture the biblical relationships, we could perhaps go back to images from the previous chapter and use a narrative adaptation of Augustine's 'memory, understanding and will'. The Father as creator 'chooses' a world in the Logos, the space of the divine imagination, and makes it real by the power of the Spirit as the conduit of structured energy, of active, divine love. (An image for this 'choosing' may be the way a scientific observation makes determinate one position for a particle whose position before was indeterminate). The weakness of this language vis-à-vis the tradition is that the divine relationships are now portrayed as three faculties of one being, rather than as the three inter-relating persons of which the one Godhead consists.

New language can only get us so far.

The God-man relationship

Such analogies are, of course, of less help when trying to make sense of the relationship between the Divine Son and Jesus of Nazareth. If Jesus exists as a real man, then he has as much of a base in the matter-energy of this world as any other man. He needs nothing else to individuate him. It could be argued that his matter-energy is sustained by the energy of God, but that would be true of the whole of creation as well on a traditional understanding.

The relationship could, however, be conceived as a particular act of new creation according to the shaping power of the Word. This takes as analogy the general relationship of God as creator to the whole universe. Jesus' material-energy is *separately* implanted in the world, obeying the same rules, still fully human but uniquely emergent from, shaped by and in relationship to the informing Word. On this model, Jesus the man, in unique relationship to the divine Word, would represent a new creation from conception. This may raise problems regarding his solidarity with the rest of humanity, which is the product of the existing energy of the universe. There are also implications for the traditional theology of Mary.

The traditional language concentrated on the unity of the divine and the human at the level of physical reality or individuation. So far we have adopted a similar approach. Yet again, as human beings, we might be more interested in the *psychological* unity of the divine and human selves, as knowing, experiencing, loving subjects. The problem here is twofold. First, the tradition insists that the two psychological selves belonging to each nature are distinct. They are in relationship, but they are never merged. Secondly the only reliable way we humans can identify psychological subjects as single is by tracking the bodies they occupy through space and time. What does it mean for two selves to be one person – how can that happen? And then, if there are two selves in one individuating reality, how can they be genuinely two.

We want to say he is truly God. We want to say he is truly man. We want to say that he is not two distinct entities, preserving different experiences and trajectories from the moment of union. We can begin to construct new pictures and new analogies that harmonise with the world as we presently understand it. But there is more imaginative work to be done here and the imagination needs to be in harmony with contemplation.

Chapter 4   A History of the Soul

'And many of those sleeping in the hollows of the earth will be raised up, some to everlasting life, some to reproach and to everlasting shame' Daniel 12, 2.

'The soul' is a vital concept for theology. It not only reflects our understanding of our nature and destiny as human beings and perceiving subjects, but also provides an analogical base for our concept of God as non-material spirit. The Jewish and Christian philosophers of antiquity readily made use of models of the soul proposed by Plato, the Stoics or Aristotle, according to which it was easily possible for the soul to exist independently of the body and to be re-embodied, as the scriptures required. Once again, however, modern thought forces us to look anew at the received opinion. Neuroscience and modern philosophy of mind challenge our intuitive understanding of the relationship between mind and brain. Psychology and sociology alter our understanding of the unity and identity of the human self. This raises problems for a faith which insists on the reality of personal survival after death. It also undermines our analogical base for talking about God.

We will begin, as before, with a sketch of the origins of the language of 'soul', look at the modern difficulties and suggest some pointers towards a new way of talking in harmony with the tradition.

It is quite common nowadays to contrast one of the Old Testament words for the self, 'nephesh', with the Greek word most commonly used to translate it, 'psyche'. The Hebrew word is more closely tied to the body, it is argued, while the Greek word refers to a reality which can be separated from the body. The Greek terminology, by implication, downgrades the body (perishable) and leads to the hostility towards it which seems to characterise some Christian writing and ascetical practice. Because this seems self-evidently bad, the scriptural 'nephesh' is often preferred to the Greek 'psyche' as a guide to understanding what we are before God.

Unfortunately, the relationship between the words is a little more complicated than this line of argument implies. The use of 'nephesh' in the various books of the Old Testament does often imply fluid boundaries between physical and psychological states. However, most of the Hebrew scriptures appear to have been written in an era before there was much theological interest in *personal* survival after death. References to survival after death characteristically contrast the living, who are able to worship and praise God, and the dead who belong to Sheol and cease to count in the eyes of God. If there is anything left of the self afterwards, it is of no great consequence.

We saw earlier that there are passages in Isaiah (8th/6th century) and Ezekiel (6th Century) which speak about rebirth from death and life restored, but I argued that these are ambiguous. They appear in contexts in which the prophet is talking about the restoration

63

of the people to their land at the end of the Babylonian exile of the 6th Century. The motif of a return to life is thus, in context, more naturally read as a metaphor for the restoration and rehabilitation of the people of God in a new relationship with him.

Unambiguous references to life beyond death and the vindication of the just first appear in writings of the Greek period. We find them in the book of Daniel (2nd Century) and the books of Maccabees and Wisdom (1st Century BCE) as well as in a large amount of unofficial religious literature from the same period. It is at this point, I suggested earlier, that those ambiguous texts from the older prophets and the Psalms were being widely reread as texts about an afterlife and a new creation.

We can recall that Josephus, in his description of 1st Century Jewish groups refers to Pharisees, who believe in the resurrection of the body (for the just), Essenes, who (at least according to Josephus) believe in the survival of the soul, but do not believe that the soul receives a new body, and Sadducees, who do not believe in an afterlife at all. Then in the New Testament there are glimpses of contemporary debates in John 12 (the raising of Lazarus), in Mark 12 (the debate with the Sadducees) and in Acts 23 (Paul's speech before the elders in Jerusalem).

Belief in the afterlife seems to be associated with a Judaism of 'protest'. The book of Daniel itself was written during the difficult years of the resistance to the Greek overlords. Belief in the afterlife and in a new world is clearly linked to martyrdom in Maccabees: bearing witness to God's truth at the cost of one's life. It is most probable that the groups of 'pious ones' who were at the forefront of the defence of the faith were the forerunners of those who later became identified as Pharisees and Essenes. But significantly, some of these appear to have continued their protest, even after the Greeks were banished.

The reason for this seems to have been that, even though the Maccabees had led the resistance, they should not have been allowed to rule as High Priests because they were not descended from Aaron. The Qumran sect under the teacher of Righteousness and others – perhaps including some of the Essenes and the early Jewish Christians – therefore maintained a protest in different forms against a corrupted Temple and an inauthentic leadership.

In contrast, the Sadducees seem most closely aligned with the political authority in Jerusalem. Their vision of their faith consists in the preservation of the Temple-based cult and obedience to the Torah. In the New Testament period this pragmatic leadership co-operates closely with the Roman authorities. It is unlikely to be an accident that they do not accept the writings of the prophets as scripture, since other groups are reading them as texts which criticise the leadership and look towards a new order. The very concept of an age to come, to which belief in the afterlife is closely tied, implies a challenge to the existing religious and political order.

Again, it is not surprising that after the final removal of Jewish authority from Jerusalem after the Bar Kochba revolt in the 2nd century CE, the Sadducees disappear from the scene as their reason for existence disappeared with the destruction of the Temple and the Jerusalem aristocracy. The dominant strands of Judaism which emerge from those years under the leadership of the Rabbis preserve the radical tradition of belief in the afterlife.

Interestingly there seems to be little sign of the modern concern over dualism which we mentioned at the beginning. In one of the medieval mystical writings of this Jewish tradition is found the phrase: 'The soul (nephesh) is separated from the body as easily as a hair is drawn from milk'.

Jewish belief in the afterlife and the wider world

I argued earlier that this apparently independent development within Judaism was more likely to have been stimulated and continuously affected by interaction with the wider Hellenistic world. I suggested that Josephus may well have been accurate in making a connection between Pharisaic and Stoic beliefs, between the style of the Sadducees and the philosophy of Epicurus. Following on from that argument, I should like to show how Stoic doctrine could be used to provide a rational framework for a scripture-based belief in the resurrection of the dead.

The Stoics do not appear to have thought of the soul as a different sort of thing from the rest of the universe: it simply belongs to one of the four elements (fire), whose proper place is in the heavens. The Stoic soul is thus a part of the fabric of the universe and its interaction with the other element when it exists in an earthly body does not pose any problem. Nor is there a problem with its existing independently and going to its 'natural' place with the stars when it is separated from the body at death. At the end of a cycle of time, the cosmos is consumed in flames, everything is regenerated and a new version of history begins, with the souls once more restored to bodies.

Against such a conceptual background, it is easy for a Greek-speaking Jew to show a non-Jew how his scriptures speak of the spirit of God breathing on dry bones and raising them to life; or how God speaks through the prophets and says 'behold I make all things new'. This reading of those texts 'fits' the scientific world view of the Stoics. It is no accident that the heavenly journey described in the (late) non-scriptural book of 2 Enoch implies a Stoic or Aristotelian cosmology and locates the encounter with the souls of the dead in the heavens, rather than below the earth. Faith and reason are in harmony. The doctrines of faith, teased out by reflection on scripture are justified by what counts as the good science of the day.

Other views on the soul and the afterlife: Epicurus, Aristotle, Plato

This is, however, not the only model of the soul available in the ancient world. Epicurus also proposes a material soul, which is, however, constructed of atoms. Its atoms are finer than those of the rest of the body but, like those of the body, they dissolve on death. Was this the understanding of the Sadducees? Josephus expressly makes the link and the New Testament picture of the Sadducees supports it.

For Aristotle (favoured by the Jewish Aristobulus), the soul is the principle of movement in an animal or plant – movement including growth and respiration as well as displacement and action. This part,

67

including the discursive thought of human beings, cannot be immortal, because it changes, and what changes, by (Aristotelian) definition, comes to an end. Aristotle does, however, allow that the contemplative part of the soul may be immortal, because truth is eternal and therefore contemplation of truth does not imply change.

Plato (favoured by the Jewish Philo) has a number of different discussions on the soul, arguing for its immortality and accepting the doctrine of reincarnation. For him the soul is non-material, being at a bridge between a world of the senses (the material world) and a world of absolute, changeless realities (the forms). The highest function of the soul, the 'logos' or reason (intellect), is able to attain to a contemplation of those realities by abstraction from the world of the senses. However, the soul is hampered by the various desires and drives arising from the body and the world of the senses, which can lead it away from the truth. The logos is assisted in its efforts to control these desires by an emotive force, which Plato labels 'anger'. Interestingly, Plato does not suggest that the logos should crush or negate the desires, but rather bring them into harmony with the higher reality, which is fundamentally an ethical reality and which has an attractive power of its own.

Plato is not as interested as others in the physical structures of the world or questions of the relationship of soul to body. With his philosophy-science he does not need to be: for him the material world or the world of the senses is not even as real as the self perceiving that world. In fact, to reach truth, the soul has to escape from the prison and illusion of the world of the senses.

Plato's image of the ascent of the mind from the world of the senses to the world of the absolute realities and the contemplation of goodness has been very influential in the history of Jewish and Christian spirituality. The book of Wisdom and Paul's letter to the Romans both refer to the possibility of knowing God by contemplating his works, and Anselm's famous argument begins with just such an ascent from lower order to higher order being. Even 'Via Negativa' spirituality (the 'negative way' or 'way of denial' as represented by the 'Cloud of Unknowing') which discards form, image and definition in the approach to God, still uses the image of the ascent, merely taking matters one rung higher.

Thus for intellectual Christians, Plato offers a basis for understanding the relationship between Soul and the absolute, and the meaning of prayer and meditation. There is a connection between the higher world of ultimate realities, the forms, and this world of shadows. The shadows in some way *participate* in the higher reality. This talk yields a theory of liturgy as a means for the faithful community to ascend, via the earthly words, images and actions of the liturgy, to participation in the heavenly realities which they represent. Plato's writings offer a first philosophy-science of Spirituality.

Though Plato appears to have accepted reincarnation, the vision of supreme happiness which he offers is a very disembodied contemplation of the forms. Aristotle too, as we have seen, considers contemplation of truth the final goal of the soul. Christian writers like Augustine and Aquinas accept this understanding of the fulfilment of the self, and see in the Beatific Vision of God the final purpose of creation and redemption. However, this model of eternal happiness can find itself neglecting the philosophical awkwardness of the bodily resurrection affirmed in the Creeds and drawn from a Jewish tradition with Stoic echoes.

The human soul as an analogy for God

These philosophical approaches to the soul do not just suggest a model for our humanity. They also provide material for a concept of God. The 'logos' (originally from Heraclitus in the Greek tradition) becomes the ordering principle of the universe, the divine Wisdom in Philo, in John and the Greek Christological tradition. Augustine uses non-Platonic psychology to explain the Trinity as 'memory, understanding, will'. The non-material human mind provides an analogical base for conceiving the non-material, supreme, intelligent, personal being.

Problems for soul and the self in the present day

But for us there are problems. In the last four hundred years, neglected ancient debates have been revived and refined. Can we know anything which is not in some way dependent on the evidence of our five, physical senses? For many people, ultimately influenced by the arguments of David Hume and of Immanuel Kant, the answer is no. Our primary reality still consists of the thoughts and ideas in our head and the world of our senses is secondary, but we have no access to a world of super-realities, a world of forms. There are no 'eyes of our mind' to see beyond the physical world. There are just images inside our heads, which ultimately derive from the objects of our senses. God, defined as a transcendent, non-sensible being is unknowable. If he is unknowable, then he might as well not be there.

Further, the concept of a world of forms is incoherent (Plato criticises the idea, annihilatingly, himself). We have become aware of how the boundaries of our concepts (political, social, ethical and scientific) change and develop through time and across cultures. If our concepts evolve continually, how can there be any absolutes to attain to?   If there are no absolutes, beyond what the consensus of human reason produces at particular times and particular places, what need is there to speak of a God as guardian or embodiment of those absolutes?

While philosophical arguments place limits on the scope of human knowledge - which effectively make faith in a transcendent being non-rational - evolutionary theory proposes that human culture and consciousness, which we regard as primary realities, are in fact second-order phenomena, products of the material world. We, as persons, have no more absolute value than the others entities in the universe, and moreover our death is necessary for the sifting of genes and the future progress of the species. In our era Epicurus and Democritus have their revenge on the Platonic and Aristotelian centuries. It is Democritus' atoms, forming worlds in the infinite void, and Epicurus's portrayal of a fragile human existence, searching for momentary happiness but ultimately subject to chance and death, which today win the battle for hearts and minds.

Finally, Freudian theory offers a model of the soul which turns Plato's upside down. The logos becomes the ego, anger becomes the super-ego and the desires disappear beneath the surface. But now, when things go wrong, it is the ego that is at fault. The determining reality of mind is not reason – all desires, thoughts, actions can be rationalised – but the hidden drives beneath the surface. In an instant, all our philosophising and theologising is undermined. All objects of philosophical and theological imagination, as products of fantasy, and therefore of the unconscious, are subject to deconstruction. The psychological 'cause' of an idea is a better guide to its value than any philosophical reason for accepting it. The conscious self that we think of as our true self is secondary to the deeper self of drives and desires. Salvation is to be sought not in a truth out there, nor in eternal happiness (a projection of our fantasy) but rather in avoiding harmful tension in the depths of our hidden selves. Far from the mind's providing an analogical base for conceiving God, the concept 'God' is reduced to an involuntary projection of the troubled mind.

The arguments of Hume and the theories of Darwin and Freud permeate our culture and affect the way we engage with matters of faith. They make it difficult for modern people to believe. Yet interestingly, neither Darwin's nor Freud's theory could actually withstand a thoroughgoing sceptical critique in the style of Hume - indeed few scientists could work with Hume's level of scepticism. But more importantly, however fruitful each of the two theories has been over time (Darwin has probably done better than Freud), it is not possible to demonstrate that either theory provides a complete explanation of the origin of life or the nature of human consciousness. Many may indeed *accept* the explanations they provide as sufficient, but that is not the same as *showing* them to be so. Thus although these ideas shape our intellectual reflexes and make it difficult to talk about the transcendent without feeling simple-minded, they cannot make it actually irrational to discuss God and the soul from a faith perspective. They are not the real problem.

Neuroscience, philosophy of mind and the survival of the self

The genuinely hard problems arise in the attempt to define the relationship between mind and brain. Neuroscience shows how different categories of mind-event, down to the religious experiences of meditation, correlate with electro-chemical activity in different parts of the brain, how brain chemistry affects mood, behaviour and thought-patterns. Conscious awareness arises with ripples of activity taking place throughout the brain. The memories that are so vital for our sense of continuous self are stored in a brain uniquely shaped by our experience in this body.

But what exactly is the correlation between events in the mind and events in the brain? Could there be a thing called a soul that was separable from the brain, a non-material reality? Or should the mind be identified with the brain as a different aspect of the same phenomenon? After all, when my computer throws up on the screen the words I write, the words which I read are identical with the electron patterns created by the cathode ray tube. A 'meaning' event is identical with a physical event.

The evidence so far advanced – for want of any compelling evidence to the contrary – suggests that the psychological self is inseparably bound up with a particular brain, in a particular body, developing in relationship to a particular human community in a particular place and time. My mental self is essentially connected with my physical history.

But there are further arguments about the nature of that self. One school of thought sees the uniqueness of that brain as the basis for the unique sense of self in human self-consciousness. The awareness and self-awareness of the perceiving and thinking subject and how things appear to be to that subject are, however, phenomena in their own right (Searle). The twin awarenesses are the result of an evolutionary process which produces increasingly sophisticated self-organising systems, of which self-consciousness is the most sophisticated emergent phenomenon. A variant on this suggests that matter may have an intrinsic potential for consciousness, which is realised in the higher levels of organisation in animal life (Nagel). The sense of self and the world cannot, however, be broken down and explained in terms of more primitive physical events.

Another school of thought (Dennett) sees the self as an illusion. What happens in the mind is essentially information-processing, using the hardware of the brain. A thousand and one 'sub-programmes' have evolved to help complex creatures cope with a complex environment.

74

Consciousness is an illusion, an accidental by-product of processes which would continue whether the agent was self-aware or not.

Interestingly, this latter theory, by defining a particular psychological individual in terms of information-processing, implies that that self could theoretically be replicated if the necessary information were transferred to alternative suitable hardware. We gain thereby a theoretical immortality of the self - or rather, of a particular collection of self-organising information processes. If we were looking for a way to translate the doctrine of life after death into our present range of understandings of the universe, this would be one possible line of inquiry. The price is that we make our everlasting selves in the image and likeness of our machines.

The previous set of theories is in some ways more attractive. These insist on the irreducibility of the subject's experience of themselves and their world and they also make a necessary link between a particular self and a particular body. By doing this, however, they would also seem to preclude the continuation of that self beyond the lifespan of the body in which it has grown. How could this self survive without the body-brain that generated it, given that the self is numerically identical with that body-brain?

Claims of near-death experiences suggest that when vital functions are lost, the subject can continue to be self-aware and aware of place, persons and movement independently of the normal physical senses. However, the evidence - necessarily first person accounts - is open to more than one interpretation. Some aspects of near-death experience can be reproduced under experimental conditions where there is no question of life-functions being lost. Further, the concept of awareness without sensory apparatus to interact with the environment is not one we can easily make sense of. Nevertheless, this is the closest we are likely to get to evidential support for the idea that a soul can survive beyond death.

The image which accounts of near-death experiences provide, suggests a journey of the soul which is continuous with the self's experience so far – that is to say, takes place on the same timeline. The self continues as a form of organised energy independently of the body, which could be viewed as the womb in which this self has grown and from which it is separated for the next phase of its existence. But in this universe? If so where? Is the kingdom of heaven to be found on a distant planet? And what about the doctrine of the resurrection body? Paul does, of course, say that the new bodies will be spiritual, immortal ones, rather than fleshly, mortal ones. We need to suppose a new mode of existence and a new environment in which to exist in this way – and here the boundary between doctrine and science fiction, which seems so clear when we read ancient texts, suddenly - and disturbingly - disappears, when we try to be modern.

But again, we need to take risks if we are to recover something as central to traditional Christian belief as the survival of the self beyond death. Here, then, is some science-fiction which tries to do justice to some of the different elements in the discussion so far. It takes as its starting point the position that the mind is numerically identical with the brain, because this is where the philosophical consensus seems to tend and because it is the more difficult position for traditional

Christianity to deal with. Bear in mind that this is not the only possible approach to the question.

A modern journey of the soul

Let us suppose that the soul of the human person does indeed grow with the body and ceases to exist at death on the ordinary timeline. But let us also assume that the soul-body, which is finite along the normal timeline, also exists on another timeline, running perpendicular to the entropy timeline of the universe. Death brings about a change of consciousness. The person is still embodied, and the embodiment is continuous with the earthly body. The consciousness is continuous, but it is consciousness of existence on a new timeline, which is completely present to every moment of existence on the entropy timeline (earthly existence).

At this point an analogy from Physics may help. The position of a particle like an electron moving in a fixed orbit around a nucleus is expressed in the Schroedinger equation. But what the equation yields is not fixed positions at fixed points in times, but a probability of where the particle is at any one moment. The equation, a wave equation, expresses all the points that the particle could occupy and in the boundary metaphysics of modern science the particle 'exists' at every point permitted by the wave equation. Significantly for our metaphor, in the case of an orbiting electron, its position can be expressed without reference to time.

Thus the 'boundary metaphysics' of orbiting particles combines infinite movement (within a limit) with freedom from time. We now have space to talk of a time-free existence of embodied beings, which move and fulfil themselves eternally. The whole person is taken up into a further dimension of experience which entails a deeper presence to God, an altered presence to their own total experience and a transformation into an embodied, moving yet timeless perfection of themselves. We have the beginnings of an alternative to the more sedentary and disembodied beatific vision.

This approach is not without its problems. Is eternal happiness an awareness of myself climbing every possible mountain or living every possible life? What about the new physical order implied in the tradition of the new creation? What about the causal relationship between the self of the life I have worked through and the life to come? Perhaps there are other models for the journey of the soul into a richer space-time of which our this-worldly experience is only a part.

'Time', 'timelessness', 'eternity', 'movement' and 'forever' raise huge problems for the imagination. They will now be developed in a supplement to this section, which includes a discussion of the relationship between divine action and human freedom.

Chapter 5: Time and Freedom

There is an ancient difficulty in reconciling God's complete knowledge of the world, his all-powerful control of its destiny with human freedom and responsibility. If God knows everything that we are going to do, how can we do anything to change it? If God is in ultimate control of whether we accept or reject him, how can we be blamed for rejecting him, and in what sense can we deserve hell? Augustine treats of these matters in his Handbook of Faith, Hope and Love. For him, the narrative of redemption in Christ is closely tied to the narrative of human responsibility. His treatment incorporates the language of predestination which is found in many of the New Testament writings and emphasises the sovereignty of God's grace, perhaps at the expense of human freedom.

I want to suggest an alternative way of thinking which allows God to be omniscient about history without implying determinism. Then I want to suggest a way of supposing a free, gracious action of God which is compatible with a real human freedom. In order to do this I want to make use of two 'boundary metaphysical' concepts which take us beyond our everyday observed reality, but which have proved useful to scientists in making sense of that reality. The first concept is that of observer-relative time, borrowed from Einstein, and the second is that of imaginary time, borrowed from Stephen Hawking and, indirectly, from Augustine and Plato.

We experience an unfolding universe and ourselves as part of it. Each of us occupies a tiny segment of the timeline of the universe, the succession of its events, as it either expands towards a cold infinity or oscillates back towards a fiery collapse. From our point of view, the past is determinate and the future is indeterminate.

Let us now suppose an observer who exists on a timeline (o-time) parallel to the timeline of the universe (u-time). Every point in o-time corresponds to a point in u-time and at each point the being in o-time observes the totality of events in corresponding u-time. For this observer the past is determinate and is remembered, the present is determinate and directly known, but the future is indeterminate, because it depends on actions of free beings like us which are not yet known. Notably, knowing what choice someone has made does not render them unfree in that choice.

We further suppose that the history of the universe is complete. The history, which also includes the history of our free choices is now determinate. The observer in o-time has known directly every event at every moment of u-time without affecting the freedom of choice of beings like ourselves. The observer has a direct present knowledge of the final state of the universe and a memory of all the previous states.

We now suppose that o-time slows down, relative to the totality of u-time, so that the interval between the first and final observations of the universe shrinks towards zero. This is most easily seen by a diagram.

```
o1      o2      o3      observer time          o1        o2        o3
o1'     o2'     o3'     observation time              {o1'o2'o3'}

 |       |       |                                        /|\
 |       |       |                                       / | \
 ↓       ↓       ↓                                      ↙  ↓  ↘
u1      u2      u3      universe time          u1       u2       u3
```

Case 1: The o-time of the observer is the   Case 2: The o-time of the
     same relative to u-time   observer slows down
                                            relative to u-time and the
                                            interval between the first
 and last observations of
 the universe tends towards
 zero.

In case 2, from the perspective of the universe, the observer does not change. From the perspective of the observer, the history of the universe passes in an instant.

Such variations in relative time between observer and observed are predicted by the theory of relativity and discovered in experiment as one or other approaches the speed of light.

In the second case, where the interval between the first and last o-time observation approaches 0, the observer's knowledge of the universe becomes direct present knowledge of every moment of u-time and the need for memory disappears. None of this, however, has any effect on the freedom of subjects living and choosing in u-time.

This gives us a model for how God can have complete 'timeless' knowledge of the history of the universe while we still have real free choice.

But we also want to suppose that God acts graciously in response to human choices and in anticipation of them. We want to suppose that God holds the ultimate destiny of the universe in his hands. In this case, we need a new timeline for God to map the sequence of his reactions to events in u-time that spring from free human choices. God observes the totality of the universe before she reacts on this timeline and each intervention in response to human choice represents a change of direction for the universe. This time, in which God acts, we label z-time. Remember that this is specifically for the cases where a free choice is being made on the timeline of the universe which takes the universe in a direction away from the one God wills for it. Z-time allows God to make her move to bring the universe back into a closer harmony with her will in a cosmic game of chess (to use the analogy of Peter Geach).

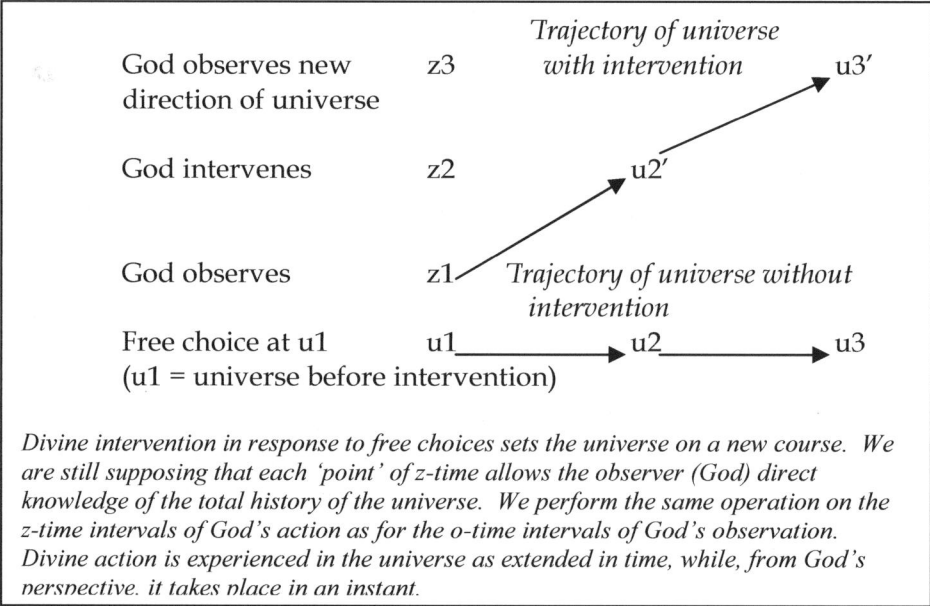

God observes new direction of universe $z3$ *Trajectory of universe with intervention* $u3'$

God intervenes $z2$ $u2'$

God observes $z1$ *Trajectory of universe without intervention*

Free choice at $u1$ $u1$ $u2$ $u3$
($u1$ = universe before intervention)

Divine intervention in response to free choices sets the universe on a new course. We are still supposing that each 'point' of z-time allows the observer (God) direct knowledge of the total history of the universe. We perform the same operation on the z-time intervals of God's action as for the o-time intervals of God's observation. Divine action is experienced in the universe as extended in time, while, from God's perspective, it takes place in an instant.

We now perform the same operation on z-time as we did on o-time and allow the time interval between God's first and last intervention to approach the limit of zero. We have a model for how the timeless, all-knowing God can intervene timelessly in history without prejudice to human freedom. We choose freely, while God leads us and the universe towards salvation.

There are weaker and stronger interpretations of z-time. On the weak understanding, z-time is simply there to capture the sequence of free decision, observation and response. It is simply a more differentiated version of o-time, which runs 'parallel' to the time of the universe. On this understanding, there is only one real universe, which is continually shaped by God's intervention.

The stronger version of z-time supposes that God cannot act definitively unless he knows the end outcome of any given set of free choices in any given universe. Thus z-time contains a real succession of universes upon which God can act *at any point* to achieve a determinate result. As z-time approaches zero (timelessness) these universes, with histories which grow towards salvation, in some sense coexist. If we wanted to picture z-time in relation to the timeline of the universe, we would draw it perpendicular to u-time. In this version of z-time, the history of the universe is plastic in the hands of God.

This takes us into boundary metaphysics again. Some physicists have used the concept of alternative universes coexisting (in superposition) to make sense of the indeterminacy (of momentum and position) of subatomic particles. Others have used the concept of many universes when trying to explain the anthropic principle (to be discussed) without invoking God. Whether we want to use the concept of z-time (weak or strong) will depend on whether we think it helpful in making sense of the things we want to say about God and her relation to the world. Let us return to three areas where it may be helpful.

Life after death

We have already discussed the problem of the continuity of the subject after death, in particular the specific Christian problem of a continued existence in a new body. If we keep within the limits of the timeline of our universe we have nowhere to locate a re-embodied existence after death. If, however, we suppose that there is a timeline in which God acts independently of the sequence of causes and events that form the timeline of our universe, then we can begin to see how we can, as subjects, exist on two timelines at once. The first of these (the u-timeline) comes to an end in death. The second (z-time) intersects with that u-timeline of which we are conscious. We encounter it in those moments when God intervenes in our lives, moments of prayer, grace, miracle, sign, gift. Eventually, when this-worldly consciousness fails in death, the second timeline becomes the only one of which we are conscious, belonging to God and to eternity. It is the timeline in which God invites and leads us into their eternity.

Our embodied selves continue to be a part of us – our history in the universe is taken up in z-time – there is continuity of the embodied self. But there is also space for transformation of our selves as psycho-physical beings in this different timeline with its new sequence of cause-event. Thus movement, which remains important to us for our full expression as embodied beings, is present in z-time, tending towards timeless motion, as we shrink the z-timeline to an eternal point.

Timeless movement

Z-time is the timeline on which the freed self knows itself, others like it and God in a (hyper)physical existence but with a set of causal relationships 'perpendicular' to those of the limited physical existence in u-time. It may be that real extra spatial dimensions are needed to make sense of such an existence. The boundary metaphysics of string theory, whose mathematics require a many-dimensional space, at least justifies us in contemplating such an idea.

But z is also the timeline of infinite possible universes, and thus of infinite possible states of individual subjects within those universes. This may allow us to make sense of the concept that the afterlife entails fulfilment, without being troubled by the limits which our narrow aspirations in this world might place upon us or the terror of doing the same thing for ever and ever. We might suppose that the hyperphysical self can exist in an internally unbounded number of states, yet bounded externally by the character and this-worldly history of the individual. It would then seem that as z-time approached the limit of timelessness, we would find a superposition of states of the hyperphysical individual. Again we can call on the image of the bounded particle in the

Schroedinger equation to justify this language. In z-time we could experience the limitless fulfilment made possible within our bounded potential: all possible thought, motion, music, dance, relationship, timelessly present before God.

The Legend of the Fall

Death is a part of our universe, and appears to be a necessary part of it, if the theory of evolution is in large part correct. While John Hick explains the hard edges of our world as a structure necessary to us if we are to learn what it is to make real choices and to learn to choose well, Darwin and Mill find such a universe incompatible with a loving God.

The ancient explanation, found in the legend of Pandora and of the Garden of Eden, and repeated by Augustine, supposed that hardship and death were the punishment for an original act of disobedience. Unfortunately archaeology and palaeontology find no trace of a time in which there was no death, and traces of an age of simplicity and harmony are hard to come by.

The strong z-time hypothesis allows for an original universe of deathless harmony (u0) which is lost, because of the free choice of beings like us. We are thus condemned by our forerunners' choices to exist in a family of universes in which we learn to find God the hard way, in a space bounded by the realities of suffering and death.

The conflict between the logic of Grace – every event is in the hand of God – and of free will – humanity can act independently of God – is to some extent resolved. No claim is made about the purity of the human will. It is assumed that there will be a limit on human freedom to act. In part this will be due to the limited, and sometimes sinful, social structures of thought and behaviour which evolve over time and in which people learn to exercise their freedom. Nevertheless, there is space for free human responses to God's invitation. And these will not all necessarily take place within a Christian context. In the field of possibilities in the divine imagination many are the pathways that lead to God.

Space is also possible for a real interpretation of the effectiveness of prayer. It will be argued in the following section that the edges of the universe are plastic to the intentions, as in the mind-brain relationship. We might then suppose that human prayer could at least alter the field of what is possible. Second, we have supposed that God can freely operate out of z-time. Accordingly, he has the space to respond to prayer.

It is possible to see here the outline of a realist account of cooperation with Grace which steers between the Scylla of absolute human freedom and the Charybdis of practical divine determinism.

Problems with the strong z-time hypothesis.

The strong hypothesis of z-time allows God to alter the past of the universe. This then raises problems about tracking individuals across the universes in z-time. What happens to me if, in the next universe in z-time, my parents do not meet? Perhaps this implies a self-imposed limit on God's actual intervention: she cannot respond to free decisions which remove from history those individuals whose existence she has willed.

Chapter 6   Towards a Natural Theology

So far we have *assumed* that major tenets of received Christianity might be true and attempted to show how its claims can be harmonised with some of the claims of modern science and philosophy. In the next two chapters we will discuss whether it is reasonable to believe in God at all and then, in Chapter 8, develop a theory for how we might be *justified* in accepting the specific beliefs of Christianity.

There are many ways, simple and ingenious, to demonstrate the existence of God. None of these will convince anyone who firmly rejects belief in God to change their mind. What they can do, however, is show that belief in God is not unreasonable, or at least is not as unreasonable as the critical climate of our era would have us believe. There follows an adapted version of the design argument to make this point.

The Anthropic Principle and metaphysics without God

Modern physics has thrown up a curious metaphysical paradox, which it titles 'the anthropic principle'. The gist of this is that we (self-evidently) live in a universe which supports the evolution of intelligent life, yet if the structures of the universe, the constants of nature (e.g. h, c, G) or the boundary conditions at the beginning of the universe were even fractionally varied, the universe would have developed very differently and complex, intelligent life would not have emerged. There is something surprising about that fact that the one universe of which we are aware has just the right conditions to produce creatures that can be aware of it.

It is, of course, only surprising if it is indeed the only universe in existence and we have accordingly two principal options for interpreting the anthropic principle. In the first option this is the only universe, or one of a limited set, and its quality is surprising, requiring a sufficient explanation in terms beyond itself. We can reason here from our experience: when we want to come up with the best explanation for an object (like a computer) which exhibits a high degree of intelligent order and intentionality, the most probable explanation is that it is ultimately the product of human intelligence. Accordingly, we would be inclined to say that the best explanation for the existence of a structure like the universe which produces intelligence is that it is set in place by a higher intelligence. The second option is to suppose that there are infinite universes or perhaps many regions in one super-universe in which many possible variants on boundary conditions, laws and constants of nature may be found (David Hume and ultimately Epicurus are responsible for this line of argument). Only those variant conditions which support intelligent life could be known by intelligent life. Thus there is nothing surprising about the nature of the universe we happen to observe.

A variant on this option extends the evolutionary model from terrestrial life to universes, imagining these emerging in bubbles out of the quantum vacuum and being 'selected' according to whether their rules sustain their own growth or cause them to collapse and disappear.

There are two things to note about these two explanations of the anthropic principle. The first is that they are both metaphysical. That is, they both posit entities which are beyond the bounds of the nature we can observe and beyond the bounds of what we can reliably test for. The second is that they represent a fundamental difference of opinion about what can count as an adequate and scientific explanation. The first option assumes that explanations in terms of mentality, intelligence and purpose are valid, even if occasionally untestable, while the second assumes that such explanations, because they are untestable, are invalid. In this view an incomplete explanation in terms of testable material-efficient causes is always to be preferred to an explanation which invokes purpose to explain coincidence. The difference of opinion has as much to do with decisions about rules of evidence as about what may or may not be true.

A modern creation narrative

Here is a version of the modern creation narrative, a complete material-efficient explanation of everything. Like all creation narratives, it is subject to revision.

The universe came into being out of a single point fifteen billion years ago. As the universe expanded with space and time (there is no space and time beyond the universe we observe) it cooled down, the energy condensed into the first particles of matter, eventually forming the simplest elements. Because of conditions that affected the initial explosion of energy, matter was not evenly distributed. This meant that matter clouds formed under the influence of gravity, eventually collapsing in upon themselves, becoming hot and dense to the point at which fusion reactions began to take place in the first generation of stars. As the stars lived out their cycle and exploded, they left masses containing higher elements, produced by the fusion reactions, to be picked up by and become the satellites of the next generation of stars.

The earth orbits the sun. It happens to contain the elements that will allow the primeval soup, rich in amino-acids to form on its surface. Complex replicating molecules emerge, which become the evolutionary forerunners of DNA, of life and, eventually, of intelligent life. The physical reality of the world is a balance of complex systems, emergent on the basic physical laws of the universe. Any change in the balance causes disruption until new systems emerge and a new balance is found in the changed environment. Intelligent life represents the culmination of a process which is built into the structure of the universe. It is the most complex system of nature of which we are aware, but, like all the others, it is sensitively dependent on initial and sustaining conditions and, like all the others, can be swept away if the conditions change. The universe is self-organising.

The theoretical bridge between the foundational explanations of elementary matter in quantum physics and cosmology and the complex systems of the biological and human realms is provided by chaos theory. This provides a mathematical basis for modelling the emergence of complexity and higher order out of simplicity without loss of causal determinism. The complex, higher-order states are sensitively dependent upon the initial conditions that sustain them. Thus a tiny variation in the initial conditions can produce a vastly different higher-order state.

The formal similarity of human choice and chaos events, and sufficient explanations - the paradox of explaining the explainer

There are, of course, actual knowledge gaps in this creation myth. No one has yet coaxed proto-self-replicating molecules out of the primeval soups around the world, but this may just be a matter of time and patience. Nor has anyone yet demonstrated the emergence of consciousness out of non-conscious matter. Computer experts are, of course, hoping for great things here. Nevertheless, if we want to, we can coherently conceive of ourselves, physically and mentally, as a collection of self-organised systems subject to laws of chaos.

Here is the problem, though. Material-efficient causality cannot distinguish between the formal structure of events arising out of human choice and events arising out of chaotic systems. Neither can be predicted by a simple formula. Only machines have the computational power to model initial conditions and trajectories in order to predict the irregular patterns of events in nature. Similar models capture with equal effectiveness the human structures of economic systems, subject not to the uncertainty of molecules but to the vagaries of human choice on the global scale. We have, then, an option of seeing in this formal continuity between the natural and the human order the true explanation, whose details are hidden from us, of what we do.

In this way we can deny the foundational reality of human meanings and intentions. Explanations in such terms belong to 'folk-psychology'. For Dennett, as we have seen, the human self is an illusion. For him any complete material-efficient explanation of human events would also be a sufficient explanation. Yet we might argue in response that to remove human meanings and intentions from our explanatory repertoire is to undermine the process of giving explanations of any kind, including material-efficient ones.

Let me put it another way. The activity of describing and explaining the universe is dependent on human systems of communication and meaning which are, for us, primary realities that can only be *sufficiently* understood in their own terms. Discredit those terms and the activities themselves become a part of the chaotic events of the universe which cannot be explained, because the activity of explaining is just another set of chaotic events in the universe.

Developing the paradox

Philosophers have approached the question from the other direction. Derrida, writing in a version of the German phenomenological tradition, points out that when it comes to the relationship between our words and the reality out there to which they refer, our concepts, words, ways of seeing the world inevitably get in the way. We never simply see things. Everything we see is already interpreted, it is a sign and what it points to is always another interpreted thing, another sign. We always see things *as* a something.

But because they have already been interpreted a world-out-there, independent of our interpretation, is not accessible to us. The argument has its roots in Immanuel Kant's proposal for understanding all human experience or knowledge as sense-data organised and interpreted by the knowing subject under pre-existing categories.

In this argument, reality 'out there' as it appears to us is distinct from reality 'out there' as it really is. This second reality might be treated as identical with the first, but is strictly unattainable.

Experimental science adopts a pragmatic approach to this question for the most part. Theories and models are tested by experiment. Some fail the test, but some are fruitful, being internally coherent, relating well to existing reliable theories and having predictive power. Such theories and models take us way beyond the world accessible to the senses to supposed realities and laws which can only be expressed in mathematics. The justification for claiming that the body of scientific theory represents a convergence on the truth of the reality out there is that experiment and technology alter reality as we experience it in ways that the theories successfully predict. It is a good working hypothesis that the reality of human experience and the reality of scientific theory are linked by a reality out there which is congruent with both. The theories approach the limit of the world as it really is.

This bridge, which takes us over the great divide of Kant and his successors, is constructed of human concepts, expressed in words, formulae, diagrams and is related to human observation. But however successful it may be in predicting events, it remains a human narrative about reality, told by humans to humans and can only ever claim provisional accuracy. Physicists are acutely aware of this problem, because, at the sub-molecular level of experiment, human beings alter what they observe. There is a still a necessary barrier, logical and physical, between our model of the world and the world as it actually is.

Earlier we gave a brief account of the scientific myth of the origin of the universe. Based on a blend of precise observations at discrete levels of reality, and using the higher-order concepts of evolution and chaos, it is able to suggest that a complete material-efficient explanation of everything, including ourselves, is possible. We reason by induction: because the material-efficient explanations have been successful so far, further material-efficient explanations will be successful in the future, with the result that, in the end, the whole history of the universe, including our human history will have a complete material-efficient explanation.

But it should be clear from the argument so far that that promise of completeness is strictly, logically impossible. There is a necessary gap between our description of the world and what we are attempting to describe. It is thus doubly paradoxical to explain the activity of describing the world in terms which eliminate the subject offering the explanation. The subject (and its immediate perception of the world) has a logical priority over the theories it generates and the only way it can write itself out of its own script is to stop writing.

The 'ordinary' life limitations of material-efficient explanation

In practice, material-efficient causality, while setting and explaining boundary conditions for human behaviours would not normally be invoked to explain individual behaviour events. Why does James have breakfast at 8:30 rather than 7:30? We look at the pattern of James' sleeping habits and breakfasting habits, do some statistical modelling and conclude that though he normally eats at 7:30, there is a random pattern of aberrations from this norm. This is because James' behaviour is sensitively dependent on initial conditions. But did James get to bed an hour later last night? Did he remember to set the alarm? Or was the next day not a working day? And so on. The statistic cannot tell us the difference between a chaotic event, a random event or a human choice.

We might, as has been suggested, be tempted to say that there is no difference. But this ignores the fact that in the primary world of human subjects and their relationships with each other there is a complex apparatus for explaining and predicting human behaviours which are statistically random. Concepts like desires, intentions, beliefs and so on can be dismissed as folk-psychology by information theorists, but they are extraordinarily useful in helping us survive on a daily basis with our fellows. They provide explanations which match the observed phenomena, have considerable predictive power and are considerably simpler and less time-consuming than running computer-modelling programmes.

97

The better I am able to appreciate the beliefs, desires, hopes and fears of those with whom I live, the more easily and happily will I make choices about how to speak and how to act. There can be no science of human behaviour (which is irregular) in the way that there can be science of a Newtonian particle. Experimental science relies on fundamentally deterministic patterns in nature which can be repeated to order, but human behaviour does not fit that pattern. Accordingly, as long as we have a practical theory of human behaviour which has useful and sufficient predictive and explanatory powers, we might want to refine it with insights from psychology, brain-science, information theory and sociology, but have no good reason to replace it with these.

The importance of 'mental' categories in providing sufficient explanations for certain classes of event in our experience

The whole argument so far has been set out to establish what is obvious in everyday terms: that explanation in terms of the purposes of individuals and groups is as real as explanation in terms of atoms and molecules. Things happen because of us which would not otherwise take place and, without invoking the apparatus of imagination, planning, intention, we cannot provide a sufficient explanation for why human artefacts, things never seen before, come into existence. The best explanation for the appearance of a set of traffic lights in the middle of a country lane includes the imagination, needs, purposes and activities of subjects like us. The process which leads to the appearance of this new sort of thing can be described from beginning to end in terms of material-efficient causality, but in this case clearly, even when the material-efficient explanation is complete, it is not sufficient.

To sum up so far: there is a class of physical reality (human behaviour and artefacts) which is properly explained by reference to the imagination and intentions of active subjects. Alternative explanations which neglect this dimension are incomplete. General theories which exclude this sort of explanation by removing the subject from its privileged position are incoherent. Without the intelligent subject, there is no explaining of any kind at all.

Choosing the best explanation of the anthropic principle

We now return to the anthropic principle and its two interpretations. The first supposes that the best explanation for the existence of structures and processes that produce intelligent life is that there is an intelligent, imaginative and purposing subject responsible for those structures. This is supported by the incoherence argument that we have just elaborated.

The second version supposes an infinite number of universes or regions of the universe, with an infinite number of variations on the basic laws, constants and initial conditions. However, this can only be a sufficient explanation if it excludes human subjectivity as a primary reality. This means rejecting the incoherence argument that has just been advanced and accepting our status as epiphenomena, whose experience and understanding of ourselves entails a high degree of illusion. Some, as we have seen, are prepared to do this.

If that 'incoherence' argument is rejected or ignored, a decision about which interpretation to choose becomes almost a matter of taste. The criteria for good scientific explanation, designed for the experimental context, cannot provide even reliable probabilities when applied to boundary metaphysics. Internal coherence and simplicity here take on a special significance – but both interpretations have their incoherencies and both are complex:

1.   It is hard to make sense of an infinite number of universes with an infinite number of variants on the laws and constants. For a universe to function its constants need definition. Each universe's constants therefore occupy a fixed point on the number line. Although there are infinitely many universes, they are discrete. To say 'it is probable that such a universe should exist' is surely not a real *explanation* of why any given universe should be like this, rather than like that. Then again how could we demonstrate that an infinite number of universes actually do exist? It seems by definition unlikely that we could do so other than by hypothesis. Do we have any evidence that any other universes exist? Surely none that could be unambiguous, given that our ability to experiment is bound by the laws of our own universe.

2.   There are equally problems with God. How can we make sense of an intelligent super-being who is non-material yet able to create (possibly) and order the material of the universe in which we live?

What evidence do we have? None that could be unambiguous. Could we ever 'prove' his existence in any scientific sense? If he behaves intelligently then any behaviour which affects the universe will have the formal characteristics of randomness or chaos, which means that even if she were acting, science could not devise tests to prove that she was doing so.

3. Which of the explanations has as its starting point the greater simplicity? The multiverse with its infinite variations and mysterious laws of generation? Or the supreme intelligent being with its infinite imagination and power? Which has the greater coherence? Which has the greater claim to being a sufficient explanation with further explanatory power?

How far does this get us?

Nothing that has been said in the preceding pages would convince a Richard Dawkins. He believes in the sufficiency of material-efficient explanation and argues that it is better science to choose the narrative which explains the emergence of complexity from simple entities and laws, than to suppose the prior existence of a more complex intelligent being that requires a further explanation for its own existence. Nevertheless, pace Dawkins, I hope to have shown that there are good reasons to think that material-efficient explanation, however thorough, cannot account for the whole of reality – that in fact it cannot even account for itself. Accordingly, I conclude that belief in God is at least as reasonable as belief in the Multiverse.

A picture of the relationship between God and the world

We have argued that the subject in relationship with other subjects is a fundamental reality in the universe, alongside the physical world we experience and the underlying physical reality supposed by science. We are entitled to go beyond the observable to make sense of why the realities which science defines and measures are as they are. In the same way, then, we are entitled to speculate about metaphysical realities which make sense of our wider experience as subjects – experience which includes love, failure, honour, shame, courage, hatred, joy, anger, despair, beauty, goodness, hope. We are entitled to use human images to explain the relationship between God and her universe, the craftswoman, the father, the husband. But we need the further support of a metaphysics, which meshes with the boundary metaphysics of theoretical science, if our thoughts are to be at peace with themselves.

We have already suggested that we can more easily understand God as an inexhaustible energy than as a necessary being. Such energy would be beyond and distinct from the limited physical energy of the universe. It would be structured in the Word, with its infinite imaginative space; in the Father, whose love provides the boundary for the Word; and in the Spirit whose power interacts with the plastic boundaries of the universe. We need to find a picture for the relationship between this transcendent energy and the universe of energy bounded by time and space.

At the fundamental level of matter-energy there is no determinism, but there is probability. The Schroedinger equation yields a probability for the position of a given particle at a given time. Particles come into being out of the quantum vacuum – from our perspective, at random – interact with other particles and then disappear. The position and the velocity of a particle do not become certain until one or other is measured. The boundaries of the universe viewed from the perspective of its basic constituents are not hard edged, but plastic, reliant for definition on something which looks, from our perspective, like chance.

But our universe develops complex, self-organising systems whose states are sensitively dependent on their initial conditions. Chaos theory explains how a tiny change in energy can be amplified and can transform the state of a system, perhaps even triggering the emergence of a new system. So if events on the edge of the universe are underdetermined, their determination can have transforming effects on the complex physical structures and events within the universe. This underdetermined edge of the universe could be compared to a computer keyboard. Press one key and a complex sequence of events is unleashed in the hardware of the computer which results in a page's being printed. Press another key by mistake and an afternoon's work is lost.

Imagine that the rather intrusive paper-clip man at the side of your screen could think. Suppose further that he worked out that he

103

and the screen display around him were the result of a beam of electrons flashing on the screen. He might ingeniously hypothesise a third dimension to explain the arrival of the electrons. He might develop chaos theory to explain the intricate structure of himself and the rest of the display. But how would he decide whether the signals coming from the keyboard came from a system in an uncertain state, that defined itself at random, or whether there was a determining cause beyond the limits of the machine?

Here is one model for the relationship between God and the world. It may also be a model for the relationship between mind and brain. God interacts with the plastic physical energy of the universe and the effect is then amplified through the higher structures. From our perspective we cannot tell the difference between God's interaction and chance. We cannot see beyond the edge of our universe and while we may reasonably claim that God exists, when trying to find words to talk about them, we can only say for sure what God is not.

Three footnotes

1.   What God is not: We say God is energy by analogy, but then we must say, but God is not energy as we understand it. That 'not-energy' is not absolute negation, which would lead us to say, perhaps she is a completely different sort of thing. Rather it is a negation that preserves the analogy. If we draw a circle on the page, we say this circle defines energy. God lies not on the inside of the circle, which we know, but on the outside, which we cannot comprehend.

2.   The plastic universe: it may not be possible to apply the position that quantum effects can be amplified by chaotic processes to large-scale events as easily as the argument suggested. The sensitive triggers for brain activity, for instance, may well take place at a level of magnitude too great for quantum activity to count.

3.   If the plastic boundary model is accepted as a way not just of explaining God-world interaction, but also mind-brain activity, then we have the beginnings also of a model which allows for the emergence of evil. Independent minds can produce structures of behaviour and example which are destructive, which resist the will of God and which place new, inner-worldly limits on human freedom. This model also allows, disturbingly, for the presence of malign intelligent forces existing within and on the boundaries of the physical structures of the universe, and which can manipulate the physical order of the universe for ill.

Chapter 7   The Problem of Evil

It is at this point necessary to say something about the basic incongruity between belief in a good God and the reality of suffering and evil. This incongruity is, after all, perhaps the most common reason cited for not believing in God. Crudely we argue that God is supposed to be perfectly good and loving, and is also supposed to be all-powerful. On an intuitive understanding of how we would operate if we were perfectly good and loving, we reason that we would do all in our power to prevent terrible things happening and being done. We also reason that an all-powerful being could achieve whatever he or she wanted. Accordingly, if the sort of God we describe did exist, there would be no wickedness and no suffering. But this is plainly not the case. We deduce that God as described does not exist. If there is a supreme being then either it is not all-powerful or it is not perfectly good and loving. In either of these cases, such a being would not be worthy of worship, as the great atheist philosopher Bertrand Russell maintained.

Traditional answers to the paradox modify our intuitive understanding of goodness, our intuitive understanding of powerfulness, or our intuitive understanding of evil. Non-traditional answers modify our understanding of God. As an example of a non-traditional approach, one can cite Roth, who presents God as a cosmic gambler, taking risks with his universe, which sometimes have disastrous consequences, though the risks are taken for benign motives.

Alternatively we could suppose, with Griffin, that God and the universe co-exist side by side throughout all time. God influences the universe, but the universe has strength to resist. Though God's shaping of the universe will one day be complete, at any point before that day there will be much happening that is contrary to God's will. This approach springs out of a theory of God from the turn of the 19th-20th Century called 'process theology'.

The traditional approaches, in contrast, preserve the received understanding of God developed over the last two-and-a-half thousand years: in this understanding it is axiomatic that God is all-powerful and all-good. It is these that I will discuss here. The dominant such approach in the Western Christian tradition has been that of St. Augustine. John Hick, in the twentieth Century, has, however, developed an alternative to that approach, which draws inspiration from a particular reading of the ancient Christian writer, Irenaeus of Lyons.

I shall begin by looking at Augustine, before presenting Hick's proposal. For while Augustine was reconciling the Biblical revelation about God, Christ and salvation with the world of ideas of his own time, his reconciliation was hugely influential in the Western Church throughout the Middle Ages and has subsequently been so in the traditions of Calvin and Luther, as well as of Catholicism. Indeed, the Augustinian world-view continues to affect discussions of sin, redemption and atonement in our own era, as we shall see in Chapter 11.

Augustine explains evil, both the (moral) evil that we do and the (non-moral/physical) evil that we suffer as the consequence of the free choice made by Adam and Eve when they chose to disobey God. Evil is, however, not a real thing; it is the absence of something – namely of good. Therefore, strictly speaking, God cannot be held responsible for evil. Through free will we, and the disobedient angels, have created an absence of good. Because of the evil done by the parents of the human race, everyone stands condemned. Whatever bad happens to us, whether through the malevolence of human beings, or through that of the evil spirits who cause natural disasters, in some sense we deserve it, along with eternal punishment in hell. God is just, and in justice we deserve to die. However, God is also merciful, and so he allows some people to be saved from condemnation. He first assists their imperfect will with his grace and allows them to repent, then when they receive his word, he assists them in living the new life offered in Jesus Christ. In this way, God characteristically brings good out of evil – and supremely so when he offers redemption through Jesus Christ as the divine answer to the sin of Adam.

There is thus no incoherence in Augustine's God. When people do bad things, they are exercising their free will and turning away from God. When bad things happen to people it is because of their guilt, and God tolerates this as punishment, because he is just. When the saved suffer, it is because they are being made more like Jesus, whom they follow. When people are redeemed and rescued from affliction or from eternal damnation, this is because God is choosing to be merciful and gracious. Either we are on the receiving end of God's justice, or we are on the receiving end of his mercy.

The easy bit is the contention that at least some of the evil in the world arises because we have free will. It seems not implausible to suppose that a world with beings who exercise free will is ipso facto 'better' than a world without such beings, even if that means that there will be evil in that 'better' world. Evil then becomes a matter of the logic of God's creative choice. She chose a world that would have free will and therefore a world that would include evil. A logical limit is placed on God's power. There is a subsidiary question: whether having freedom necessarily means that evil will come about. However, the point is that God cannot give freedom and, in the same movement, prevent its ever being used for evil purposes.

What is difficult for us is that the global set of relationships, justice, mercy, sin, salvation is dependent on a strictly literal reading of the Bible as history. Only if that global set of relationships is accepted do the notions of justice, punishment and condemnation provide an explanation for the presence of physical evil in the world. And unfortunately our understanding of the history of the universe and the rise of humanity appears to exclude the literal interpretation of the story of the fall: there was no golden age; there was no single set of parents from which all human beings come and whose sin they consequently share – quite apart from the fact that we are uncomfortable, in our enlightenment culture, with the concept of demons.

109

It seems preferable, then, to adopt an approach which does not require us to read Genesis 3 literally and yet still allows us to hold on to a traditional concept of God. John Hick's proposal gives us this middle ground. He accepts that free will is an important ingredient in the explanation of evil, but explains the divine activity in human history as a process of education, leading humanity to higher forms of understanding, to real freedom of choice and to choice of the good. God's ultimate purpose in creation is 'soul-making'. As a consequence of this divine plan, the world must be so structured that free beings can experience the consequences of their choices and so become wise. The hard edges of the world, which produce physical suffering, and which allow evil people to inflict suffering on others are therefore necessary to God's purpose. In themselves they are not evil. Neither a volcano, nor an earthquake, nor a drought, is an evil until human beings start to suffer in consequence. However, for God continually to interfere in his creation, to soften the edges of the reality used to form his creatures, would ultimately undermine his purpose. On this account, physical suffering is for growth, rather than for punishment, but is also part of the logic of God's plan, independently of questions of his power or goodness.

Thus we are not required to accept the literal truth of the stories of Genesis 1 – 3. We have a theory which fits with our common, present understanding of the emergence and transformation of human societies and cultures. The theory does not even require us to believe in

Christian redemption, just in a God who wishes to lead and human beings who can respond to that leading in this world and the next.

Understanding death

There is, however, an aspect of our world which neither of these theories adequately accounts for. Our emergence as a species requires us to die. Death is written into the script of this world. Unless the weak die, there can be no progress. In contrast, Christianity itself, the Judaism from which it comes, with its script of protecting the weak and the vindication of the oppressed, is deeply anti-Darwinian. Death is presented as an aberration, a punishment. Yet according to what most of us have been brought up to believe it is not an aberrant but a necessary part of the structure of the natural order we inhabit.

We can only then suppose that death is a now necessary part of our education into freedom, bitter though the lesson may be. We must learn how to give back to God what is God's. Only when we have done that are we ready to receive the gift of new life. Death has two aspects for us; firstly, as we travel on the timeline of this world, it is annihilation, loss, the end of everything that we hold dear. But secondly, as we discover our identity as subjects who transcend this timeline and begin to exist on a new timeline (z-time), death becomes the gateway to a richer existence in the eternity of God.

If we wanted to reinstate a version of the Adam and Eve story, we could suppose that our universe, as it is, with the hard edges and the hard lessons, ending in death, does indeed represent the outcome of our choosing the knowledge of good and evil. Perhaps the universe, with its infinite possible modulations in the timeless hands of God, had a moment, when human beings were not disobedient, did not suffer, do harm or die. In this phase of the universe there was indeed no death, no evolution. But they chose and the universe which we experience is God's timeless response to that choice. The timeline of Eden is replaced with the timeline of Darwin. The only way back is now the hard way, and that is the road humanity must learn.

Chapter 8   Knowing and Believing in God

So far the discussion has focused on reconciling some of the metaphysical claims of Christianity with the models of the physical world that are favoured by our experimental and theoretical science. We have put forward one argument, whose modest purpose is to demonstrate that belief in God is not irrational. It is now time to ask the question that lies behind belief in any particular faith tradition: if God is there, how could we find out about her?

How and what can we know?

The philosophical tradition of the West since the Middle Ages has been dominated not by the question 'what is out there?', which is the question of natural science, but by the sceptical question, 'how can I know what is out there?'. I can be reasonably sure of giving correct answers to questions about my own inner states (although this assurance has possibly been challenged by depth-psychology). However, with regard to the external world, I am reliant on the evidence of my senses. The only two worlds available to me are therefore the world of my thoughts, feelings and imaginations, and the external world mediated by my senses. It is clear that this division of human knowledge leaves no room for knowledge of beings which cannot be perceived by the senses and are distinct from the contents of my mind. There is no space here for the notion of an intuition, or contemplation of 'intellectual' realities, in the style of Plato. Nor is there

113

space for the related concept of the 'eyes of the mind' used by the mystics, which would provide us with direct images of another, higher reality.

The problem is compounded because we can give the scholastic maxim 'nihil in intellectu nisi prius in sensu' (nothing in the understanding unless first in the senses) a cash value. We can trace the mechanisms by which external reality, through electrochemical structures, alters our nervous system and so our brain. Models of psychological development explain how it is that we come to see reality under particular categories. Ways of seeing the world evolve that are useful to cultures, and individuals within the culture are taught to recognise and classify what is useful and pertinent to them. This evolved form recognition leaves its traces in the mind-brain. These traces then shape the paths of the imagination. The individual self, with its world of forms, arises out of a particular experience of physical and cultural reality. There is no space here for a mode of knowledge that could take us beyond the sensible.

Faith, and the problem of knowing the transcendent

As people who have faith in God and God's ability to communicate, we could respond in a number of ways. We could, firstly, acknowledge that we cannot 'see' beyond the forms of this world. However, we can put a positive interpretation on this. God is greater than whatever can be conceived (pace Anselm) and is therefore beyond human understanding. If we want to find God, we have to leave the forms of the world behind. God is found not with the understanding, but through the will, in the experience of love.

This line of thought lies at the base of the tradition of contemplation found in the medieval text, 'The Cloud of Unknowing'. It is the *Via Negativa* (path of negation); it reacts against the revelation tradition found in both Judaism and Christianity, with its visions and vivid portrayal of higher realities and heavenly spheres. It influences the philosopher Kant and finds its philosophical apotheosis in Wittgenstein's conclusion to the Tractatus, 'whereof we cannot speak, thereof we must be silent'.

A second, related, approach is to accept, together with the lack of concepts, the impossibility of knowledge. Religion is about feelings, and salvation comes not through knowledge (implying certainty) but through faith (commitment to that which cannot be grasped). Kant, accepting the conclusions of Hume, allows that we can have no knowledge of the world beyond the senses. We can, however, continue to have faith in such a world and in the supreme being at its heart.

A Christian empiricist theory of learning about God

A third approach can be drawn from the tradition represented by the Spiritual Exercises of Ignatius of Loyola (there are of course many other related traditions, but I will describe the Ignatian version, because that is the one I happen to be most familiar with). Ignatius invites those making the exercises to use their imaginations and memories to structure their prayer but to pay attention above all to the 'motions of the spirit', the change in the affections that takes place during prayer. Our experience has a cognitive dimension – associated with knowledge, form, concept, structure – and an affective dimension. But the emotional states of the self, its moods, relate to specific cognitive activities, ideas or images.

Our model of the 'Word as imagination' implies that there is an analogy between the world of our senses and the higher world to which we are called as more-than-physical beings. Accordingly, the forms of our this-worldly experience already contain echoes of the divine logos, and some forms will convey those echoes more deeply than others.

In this case, imaginative reasoning about the forms we have learnt to live with can theoretically lead us towards closer analogues of truth about God, better images of the way God is and what God wants of us. This is the cognitive dimension of an advance in understanding. But the criterion for affirmation – that this is towards truth, rather than empty image – is then the affective dimension of consolation, the state of joy, tranquillity, courage which for Ignatius is the mark of God's spirit acting on the human soul. There are analogies here with natural forms of successful learning, where a word of praise confirms a step in learning, and the new understanding and successful action is reinforced by delight.

On this model, communication takes place between the divine and the human, but we do not need to suppose an understanding independent of a wider human understanding developed through the experience of the world and modified and transmitted through whole cultures.

As has been discussed earlier, the forms with which we interpret our world cannot be considered as shapes clearly defined, once and for all, but as provisional boundaries implying an inner and an outer space, to be explored in the imagination. This is what makes possible the advancement of science, whose provisional conclusions and truths are constantly modified by time. Our understanding of God, who belongs as much to a world beyond our senses as quarks do, can similarly advance as one generation of analogies is developed and refined by the next.

Science is led through the success of new hypotheses towards a closer approximation to the truth – not without the occasional blind alley. Religious understanding can also be led, through the affective affirmation that is experienced in the self, towards a deeper knowledge and understanding of the absolute.

We move from provisional truths – the world is made of atoms/the physical world is a continuum – to new provisional truths which are closer to reality. Was Democritus or Aristotle right? In their way, each was right, and their imaginative science shows that it is possible to come up with a good and useful model of reality, independently of one's ability to verify or falsify it by physical experiments. It is possible to reach a truth without having all the arguments to justify it and even by deploying deficient logic. The ultimate test of a doctrine is not the route by which one arrived at it, but whether it provides a good fit for the reality it purports to describe, whether it is fruitful and coherent. This is helpful to remember when looking at the *causality* of the development of Christian teachings and when worried by poor argumentation. Equally it can encourage us in the work of re-evaluating, re-translating and rediscovering the things our tradition asks us to believe.

Towards an 'empiricist' understanding of religious experience

Let us look more closely at what being led towards truth about God might mean. We have suggested that in Ignatian spirituality there is a well-defined empirical component of religious experience, consolation and its correlative, desolation. For Ignatius, these are the means by which God, as teacher, leads the individual in choice and reinforces certain patterns of thought, images, words, behaviour. Consolation and desolation are not context free. They are about something, there is a situation: a choice is being considered, a possible future being imagined, a distinctive event is taking place, an icon is being contemplated, a word of scripture is being spoken, someone in need is being encountered, a definition is being wrestled with. Into this cognitive context, with shape, structure, form, comes the change of mode that raises the object of attention to the status of a window on the absolute. The boundaries of the experience disappear. The shape remains, but only as the medium by which the light enters the mind.

It is in this way that we can begin to make sense of the accounts of visions and of heavenly journeys. Without needing to suppose a special mode of perception, we can see how certain images or descriptions, founded on the categories of experience and related by analogy to the categories of eternity, might arise in the imaginations of gifted individuals and be affirmed by the transformation of mood that is labelled consolation. The *Via Negativa* appears *through* the *Via Positiva*.

This interpretation of religious experience relies on the theory of divine action already sketched. God as spirit acts at the underdefined boundaries of the world, specifically on the matter-self of the individual mind-brain. The religious experience is thus a physical event as well as an event in the consciousness of the individual. The interpretation further assumes that the religious imagination, which will give shape to any particular religious experience, is limited by the images and structures of the society in which the subject learns to see and talk about world and God. This point is important for thinking about some of the more gruesome aspects of salvation history in the Jewish and Christian traditions. It also, however, offers a causal account of the development of doctrine which allows for genuine development in convergence towards truth. Though every form of rationality and argument is limited by culture, it can still give life by its attempt to express the truth.

Justifying belief in the authenticity of religious experience

What we have not done is prove the reality or authenticity of religious experience. Nor have we suggested that religious experience can provide an independent proof of the existence of God. Here, the sceptical argument of Hume is valid. If the only knowledge about the

119

world beyond our heads is that which comes through the senses, then ipso facto, we cannot know a God who is not a direct object of the senses. We cannot know by looking at an event, however surprising, that God has caused it, nor can we know that a feeling within us, however powerful and remarkable, has been caused by God. The experiences are real: interior experience of consolation in imagination, the exterior experiences of a miracle or of meeting in the village street the man they say is the Messiah. But none of these experiences carries unambiguous information about its cause.

We are led back, here, to questions of choice and what we are prepared to accept as sufficient explanation. We will always be able to find physicalist accounts of remarkable brain events or remarkable natural events or of remarkable people, which will often be deemed satisfactory provided only that they promise physical completeness. But, as we have seen, such accounts cannot distinguish between the chance, the chaotic and the intentional. We have a licence to seek the more human explanations without which our account may not be genuinely sufficient.

It is therefore important to be aware of the limitation of the theory of Hume. For him all knowledge, including knowledge about forms and structures, comes through the senses. In his theory, sense data as it were force ideas and concepts upon us but in practice this is highly implausible. From the very outset of our lives we have to learn to interpret the evidence of our senses, to 'see things as'. Kant's more refined theory acknowledges that we cannot see the world without interpreting it, but does not consider the developmental and social dimension, how we learn to see. Nor does he consider how provisional our categories for understanding things may be. A strong sceptical position about our knowledge of the external world is untenable, while Wittgenstein's private language argument suggests that our ability to be self-reflective beings is dependent upon the culture in which we participate.

In fact the position of Hume and the sense-data theorists of the twentieth century reverses the way of experiencing the world which is taken for granted in folk-psychology. For us, human behaviour, affection, goodness are primary data of experience. We do not and cannot live as if we needed to be convinced by direct information that every act of kindness or generosity that we encountered was correctly interpreted as such. Our reading of events that matter to us is done against a background of experience and understandings that is far richer than the bare information from the sense data. It is against such a background and with such a justification that we might prefer to read in an experience or an encounter a sign of the action of God.

So Hume can argue that it is never rational to believe that a miracle has taken place. Miracles are, by definition, events that defy the laws of nature. The laws of nature are based on what is most usual and therefore what is most probable. To claim that a law of nature has failed is improbable and it is rational to believe whatever is more probable. Therefore it is never rational to believe that a miracle has taken place.

The argument extends to religious experience, where physical explanations for unusual mind-states can be advanced. But 'probable'

121

cannot actually guarantee truth and, more importantly, *physical* explanation, as we argued in chapter 6, cannot guarantee sufficient explanation.

The model of religious knowledge proposed above is modest. It does not require a separate mode of perception, nor does it require a divorce of the physical and the mental. It does not require the physically impossible to take place in the world. It suggests how, through images, arguments, concepts and events, human communities and individuals can be led to an ever closer understanding of who and how God is. The instrument of learning is consolation and desolation, the work of God's Spirit in human spirits.

If we want to judge the authenticity of such moments, we must look not just at their power and intensity, but at the transforming effect they have on the life of the one who encounters them. The signs of God's action cannot be read in isolation, but only against the background of the experience of individuals and the narrative of believing communities.

Chapter 9   Reading the Tradition (1)

Quod semper, quod ab omnibus, quod ubique: what has been held at all times, by everyone, everywhere. This was the old test for the authenticity of teaching across scattered Christian communities. It goes together with a particular way of understanding Christian truth, which, until comparatively recently, was an unspoken assumption in Roman Catholic teaching on faith and morals. In this understanding, the Christian texts, comprising the New Testament, the Old Testament, the traditions from antiquity and the doctrinal decisions of the Church (taken through councils or by popes) have one authentic interpretation. The history of the development of doctrine is a history of the Church identifying the correct interpretation of ambiguous texts until the point where all ambiguity is removed and all that is necessary for salvation is made clear. This history is, needless to say, linear. There are no blind alleys of interpretation and, of course, no u-turns on the way to a complete understanding of the truth. Doctrines have clear edges and the truth lies only within them.

The best of the Catholic tradition has always been more sophisticated than this, but the temptation of this way of thinking is very strong, especially in times of confusion and uncertainty. Nor can it be wrong for a community to want a common understanding of its traditions. How else are people to live, work and pray together with a common purpose? And when we look at the writings of the Old and New Testament alone, we see how great the need for authoritative interpretation is. The texts are multilayered, of many genres, the

123

products of many hands, minds, cultures, insights over a period of more than a thousand years. They are, above all, unsystematic, filled with contradictions, requiring us to make judgments about which texts are more deeply authentic, which provide the thread of Ariadne to lead us through the labyrinth. So how do we recognise the right way to read these texts, which are foundational for Christian prayer and understanding?

Interpreting sacred text – allegorical and prophetic readings

It is helpful to remember that from before the time of Christ, different groups of Jewish believers were rereading the sacred texts we label 'The Old Testament'. Intellectual Jews of the Diaspora were aware of a need to make those texts comprehensible to the hellenistic world in which they lived. A favourite method was the method of allegorical reading, itself borrowed from the stoic approach to Greek mythological texts. Thus Aristobulus is able to rationalise the theophany on Mount Sinai and demonstrate that it takes place in accord with Aristotelian principles, and Philo is able to read the journey of Abraham as an allegory for the journey of the soul to the contemplation of truth, in the spirit of Plato.

But there were other ways of rereading texts, as we see in the case of several of the Jewish groups that we mentioned earlier. The Qumran group, protesting at the corrupt priestly regime in Jerusalem, reads passages from the Prophet Habbakuk as prophecies about their leader, the Teacher of Righteousness. The texts reread in this style are not about philosophy and the world of eternal truths, but about living actors caught in a real, historical drama whose script is written by God.

It is in this style that Jesus and his followers, part of the world of 'protest' Judaism, reread the Law and the Prophets, so that, as the events of his life unfold, that life provides the key to interpreting the texts and the texts in return explain the narrative of his life. When the Christians a generation later preach the message of Jesus, they will both claim that he suffered, died and rose to fulfil the scriptures and use the scriptures to explain what his suffering, death and resurrection achieved. These are the first steps in Christian theology.

The tradition of literal/historical reading and modern critical reading

Nevertheless, in spite of this ancient readiness to read at a number of levels, there was an understanding that the historical books, from Genesis through to Ezra and Nehemiah, were to be taken on a literal level as history. The truths found in allegorical or prophetic readings of text are reliable because the text itself is in all other respects trustworthy.

This can be seen in the way Josephus writing his 'Antiquities of the Jews', first praises Moses as law-giver and historical leader and then starts his account of the history and customs of his people with a version of the narrative from Genesis, attributing this account to Moses as a respectable ancient source. This literal, historical reading of the story of Adam and Eve is found, as we have seen, in the theology of

Augustine and remained the official reading of the Catholic Church until the early years of the 20th Century.

At this point we, with our greater access to archaeological evidence and comparative literature, as well as our more sceptical approach to text, cannot accept such a literal reading without separating our believing selves from our critical faculties. And so we take a significant first step towards undermining the ancient authority of our foundational texts.

We identify different authors and styles of narrative within the so-called books of Moses. We read the account of the creation of the world in Genesis 1 and the creation of human beings and their disobedience in Genesis 2 and 3, down to the narrative of the flood in Genesis 7 – 9 as myths, similar to other contemporary myths in the Near East. We calculate that the five books of the Law were probably completed in the course of the 5th Century BC.

Whatever the authors of Genesis may have believed about their myths (probably that they represented what we would call historical truth), if we are to accept them as containing divine truth, we can only accept them as parables, showing us who we are and the nature of our relationship with God. We can only accept an allegorical reading. Yet we have already seen, in the discussion of the problem of evil, how moving away from a literal understanding of these texts threatens to undermine the grand narrative of salvation from sin and death.

When we turn to the legends of Moses, we encounter problems harmonising the claims of Exodus – Deuteronomy with comparative evidence from Egypt and the Near East. We continue to find multiple accounts of similar events, which raise questions about the account of the giving of the Law on Sinai.

We can start asking really awkward questions. Did God really say those words on Mount Sinai, or did a 6th Century author canonise a contemporary ethical catechism from the prophetic tradition by putting it in the mouth of God? Are the two tablets of the Law genuine sacred relics from an ancient act of God, or are they a way of giving an orthodox explanation to the Jewish exiles of the 6th Century of why they have a memory of two sacred slabs from the Temple(s) destroyed by the Babylonians. And when we look at two such slabs in the ancient Judaean Temple at Tel Arad in the Negev, are we looking at a representation of the tablets of the Law, or are we looking at stelai erected to a male and female deity?

Is the body of the Law itself, social and sacred, which is pronounced between Exodus 20 and the end of Deuteronomy something that was there from this historical beginning on Sinai, or is it a collection of tribal and state law, rescued from the collapse of the Northern Hebrew kingdom in 721 and edited by the priests of the Kingdom of Judah and their successors in exile, after the fall of that kingdom to Nebuchadnezzar in 584?

We may be inclined to say that the legends of Moses and the Exodus are being used as a frame for reforging the social and religious identity of a people. But this then leads us to question the powerful signs of God's saving love, the miracles. And to question these must lead us to question our whole theology.

The reasoning is simple. On the question of the miraculous signs we think like David Hume. Where testimony comes from cultures remote in time and place, in which people do not have the same understanding of nature as us and do have a greater predisposition to believe in the supernatural; when, further, the accounts are filtered through a tradition, part oral, part written of at least seven hundred years, we are reluctant to accept them at face value. In our culture and at the back of our minds, it will always be more probable that the miraculous did not occur.

There have, of course, been ingenious attempts to show how the sequence of events from the 10 plagues to the parting of the Red Sea could have taken place as the result of unusual but possible natural processes, but ultimately the problem lies not so much in the plausibility of the sequence of events itself as the route by which it comes to be reported. We are left with the following problem: if there was no miracle, if there was no act of saving love, what reason do we have to believe that God is a powerful and loving saviour?

However, once the narrative enters the Promised Land (at the book of Judges), and particularly from 1 Samuel onwards, we have much more of a sense that we are dealing with historical time. The legends concern people who leave their mark in archaeology. Parallel accounts of the same event usefully show partisan bias. Is it a good thing that the people of God should be ruled by a king anointed by God rather than a judge or prophet? Some sections of narrative support one side, some the other. Here we may be closer to things that really happened.

At one level we have a collection of narratives which trace the lives and deeds of the leaders of God's people as they move from rule by local and temporary judges to rule by kings. We read of Samuel as the last religious or prophetic leader of the tribes of Israel, Saul and the beginning of a united kingdom, David who establishes that kingdom by military strength, Solomon, who consolidates the kingdom and builds the first temple to God. We learn of the great split between north and south after the death of Solomon, the struggle between King Ahab and the prophets Elijah and Elisha, the destruction of the Northern Kingdom of Israel by the Assyrians. Hezekiah, king of Judah is rescued from Sennacherib. Josiah, king of Judah discovers the book of the Law in the Temple and institutes a religious reform. Finally, the Kingdom of Judah, too, is captured by Nebuchadnezzar, King of Babylon.

But there is a clear thread running throughout and creating the grand narrative of the Old Testament. This whole history is telling a story about God's (often stormy) relationship with his people and its rulers. Insofar as they keep her laws and decrees, they are protected from their enemies, but because they turn away, worship false gods and do what is displeasing in her sight, they are punished and their enemies triumph over them. This theology, presented vividly in the parable of Adam and Eve, is the key to reading history correctly and the history, in turn, provides evidence of the theological truth. This is the theology of the prophets, from Amos to Ezekiel, who denounce the leaders of the people for their failure to obey their God and promise as punishment for sins, historical disaster.

The prophets interpret not texts, but events, and their interpretation is justified by those same events. Their reading is taken over by the historians who create a complete narrative to make sense of the terrible events of the destruction of the Northern Kingdom of Israel (721 BCE) and the Southern Kingdom of Judah (584 BCE) by the Assyrians and the Babylonians, respectively. The blessings and curses listed in Deuteronomy explain why everything has been lost and why the people are now exiled from their own land. If they had obeyed God, they would have prospered, but because they were disobedient, they have been punished.

The voice of the prophets, speaking in history, and the cultural reality

Against that background we can place prophets in their historical context. Those whose writings date from the time of the two kingdoms speak in the name of God, calling contemporary rulers to account for false religious practices and social injustice, and proclaiming a judgment of God which will be expressed in political disaster. But then, in the period after the disaster of 584, the prophets of the Exile begin to speak with a new voice. They speak of restoration and the renewal of the covenant, of the people returning to their land. When Cyrus leads the Persians to become the new middle-eastern superpower he allows the Jewish exiles to return. In this historical reality, too, the prophets read a sign of God's work: this time of his gracious and saving work.

This prophetic reading of history does not, however, sit completely at ease with what other indications suggest may have happened. The theological history supposes, for instance, that the people began from a position of obedience to their tribal God, the Lord, worshipping him alone and keeping his commandments as given on Sinai. The archaeology suggests, by contrast, that the Lord was one God among several who were worshipped at various sacred sites throughout the region, including, eventually, the Temple of Solomon. There are hints that, until quite late in the Kingdom of Judah, two deities were worshipped in a number of temples. The history texts themselves suppose that at least from the time of Solomon there was a cultic pluralism within the kingdom.

There seems, then, to be something of a discrepancy between the continual, urgent call of the prophets and the actual practice. Given the problems with the legends of Sinai, it is unclear whether there was ever a time of pure worship of the Lord, as the prophets and the prophetic history writers suggest. On the other hand, there is evidence of religious reform, in line with the prophetic demands: the sanctuary at Tel Arad, with its two incense altars, was walled in at some point in the 7th Century, for example. More significantly the character of Judaism after the exile is quite clearly shaped by the prophetic writings of the previous centuries.

How justified is that prophetic reading of history? The scholar J. Alberto Soggin questions the historical accuracy of a relationship between obedience and success. Omri, King of Israel, denounced as one who did what was displeasing to the Lord, nevertheless consolidated his realm so effectively that it was known as 'the Kingdom of Omri' to its neighbours. Similarly, Manasseh in Judah, also denounced as one who neglects the covenant, had a long and happy reign, while Josiah, who followed the example of his ancestor David, by removing the objects of false cults and promulgating the book of the law, was killed on a disastrous expedition against the King of Egypt. His unfortunate sons, Jehoiakim and Jehoiakin, took to the throne in their teens and had just enough time to do what was displeasing to the Lord before the Babylonians came. According to the history writer, this was really because of the sins of Manasseh, which were too great to be outweighed by anything Josiah had done. Perhaps the author felt it was a little harsh to put the entire blame on the two brothers.

The problem of parables and New Testament text

This selective, theological history of the kings, then, like the legendary (Moses) and mythological (Adam and Eve) sections before it,

132

can be read as one great parable, demonstrating a theology of how God interacts with his people, giving content to the terms of the covenant and a real value to the expressions 'God saves' and 'God loves'. But again we face the same problem: if this whole history is a parable it may helpfully illustrate what we might want to say about who God is and how she is, but if it is not simultaneously real history, it is providing no evidence that what it claims is true.

Yet this history and theology are foundational for the history and theology of Christians. The writings of the New Testament continue the narrative of the saving love of God found in the older Jewish texts. The texts report as historical the events surrounding a person whose existence is not seriously disputed, but whose miraculous actions and, above all, whose miraculous resurrection from the dead are so closely bound to a very particular reading of Old Testament texts that the veracity of the accounts seems bound up not just with the reliability of the witnesses, but with the authenticity of the Old Testament tradition.

Crudely put, if the miracles of Moses are real, we can have no problem supposing that those of Jesus are too. But, correspondingly, if the miracles of Moses are not real and the Old Testament is one vast parable, why should the same not be the case with the miracles of Jesus - and with the whole New Testament? And this way lies the 'Sea of Faith' Christianity of Don Cupitt - a Christianity without God. If we must accept that some of our text is parable, we want to know how to judge the point at which parable ends and historical reality, the justification for the parable, begins.

The possibility of signs, keys to reading a history with God

Elaborate pains have been taken in earlier essays to attempt a coherent account of God's action in the world. By this account, the edges of reality in our universe are plastic and as a consequence God has freedom to interact with any situation at any moment in any way he chooses. It is therefore possible that God can cause events in accordance with the laws of nature which are, in our eyes, highly improbable. Such events can then be read by those whose eyes are opened (by God) as signs of his presence. These we would naturally call miracles. It follows that there can be many other events, of rather different degrees of probability, which can also be read as signs, though we would not necessarily call them miracles, and which form part of our common and personal history. It is by noticing such signs that individuals and a community can learn how God is dealing with them.

We must always bear in mind that this line of thought is not a proof of the existence of God or of miracles. It does, however, usefully show that it is possible to talk about encountering God in history in a way that is consistent with a modern understanding of the world. Assuming that we accept the possibility of such signs, the next question is: how are we to tell whether we are reading a sign that is there? Are we inventing significance where there is none and seeing castles in the clouds?

Here a good guide is William James' proposal for identifying an authentic religious experience, noting not just the private emotional intensity of the experience, nor just the power of the images or ideas communicated, but also the effects of that experience in the life of the subject. The reading of an event as sign is justified by its fruitfulness in the context of a whole life. Where a life is transformed in a way which is recognisably for the good, and where the sign becomes a key for interpreting other, otherwise mysterious, aspects of existence, there is the best indication of authenticity that we are likely to have. When such signs enrich the life of a whole community – which, in spite of collective failings, manages to live in creative and admirable ways that are different from the common – then the parables and the narratives of that community are worth taking seriously.

The 'proof' of the parable of salvation history is not to be sought, in the first instance, in the bare facts of a whole history, whose sign value is indeterminate until it is read. It is to be sought in the lives of the prophets, of Hosea and Jeremiah, whose passionate and personal experience of God teaches them to see his hand at work in the events of their time and gives them words to speak which they themselves perhaps do not fully understand, many of which are fulfilled despite the mockery of their adversaries. It is because of the authenticity of this personal experience, bound up with the whole experience of the community, that it is possible to read other signs out of the confusion of history. And yes, even though Hezekiah had to buy off the Assyrians, at least his throne was safe and yes, even though Josiah got killed at Megiddo, he brought the Law to the eyes of the people and won back lost territory. These were read as moments of gift for the people, moments of grace.

So maybe the Red Sea was parted and maybe it wasn't, but the memory of a time of liberation was real and the Jews who came back to Jerusalem under Cyrus to rebuild their temple understood what it meant to be led through the desert places to their own land and saw in this the hand of a loving and redeeming God.

Theology and fixing meanings: the lessons of the centuries

The experience of signs and their interpretation give us the beginning of theology. In the Old Testament it is a theology carried by the narrative of history and the preaching of the prophets, though the later Wisdom literature offers more reflection and speculation. In the New Testament it weaves around the person and teaching of Jesus Christ, the ultimate sign of the saving God proclaimed by the prophets.

Thereby we see again and again that texts, even sacred texts, do not determine their own interpretation. Later generations reread them in the light of their own experience and history. New understandings evolve out of the old. The Qumran sect finds in the writings of the prophets a protest against an unholy religious administration of the Temple, and withdraws to the desert. Jesus of Nazareth finds in the writings of Jeremiah and the prophets a call to risk death by confronting the priestly leaders of Jerusalem with a new, more deeply authentic reading of the Law than theirs. The first generation of Christians, their lives transformed by their encounter with Jesus, begin to find in the scriptures a source rich in explanation of that encounter.

Familiar words take on a new meaning and a new resonance when projected against the narrative of experience. There is a new understanding of who God is and how he, she, they lead and save the people she loves. And this God speaks to his people, through their experience, in a language that they can understand. If it is the language of politics, he will speak in battle. If he is dealing with a fisherman, it will be through an impossible catch of fish. And language is acquired and transmitted. Each generation's common experience gives the next generation a language and a practice to discover God for itself. Yet in each generation, in each person, God is encountered in a new way. God is more than the words and practices which have been passed down. Words are the window on a reality that is more than words. Precepts are a pathway towards a person, not a code.

Reading and rereading the Christian tradition

If God is real, salvation history continues. Signs of God's loving work are there to be read in the histories of individuals, peoples, nations, creeds. Christianity, too, has its own salvation history: the response in time of its leaders, its communities and its individuals to the invitation of God. For every Christian group, however, an important part of that history is the traditional teaching that has evolved through the experience and the conflict of the centuries. The teaching encompasses what a Christian should believe and how a Christian should live. The tradition is a gift. It approves a particular reading of the past as reliable and says from experience, 'here God may be found'.

In the Roman Catholic Church the tradition has had various champions. Its guardian is now known as the 'magisterium', the teaching authority of the Church, whose ultimate instance is the Pope. Throughout the centuries traditional practice and belief have been challenged by new ideas, new ways of thinking about God or of salvation. Sometimes these have come from within the Christian community, sometimes from beyond. It falls to the protectors of the tradition to defend it against things which are new and which would, dangerously, lead Christians away from the life-giving truth. Yet in that encounter with the new, the tradition itself is transformed and grows. And something richer will be passed on to the next generation.

Let us now try to read something of that tradition, specifically the Roman Catholic tradition. We will look at three things that can be regarded as distinctive of Roman Catholic Christianity: sacraments, the language of sacrifice and ethical teaching. As before, we will seek to understand the language of the past so that we can think our faith in the language of our time.

Chapter 10   Sacraments and the Eucharist

It is occasionally tempting to think that Catholic Christianity suffers from over-definition and the inherited teaching on sacraments is one area where that temptation is particularly strong. The word 'sacrament' itself *denotes* one of the canonical forms of liturgical action in which God is believed to grant his gracious action on behalf of the participating community. What it *means*, however, has passed through a number of transformations in the history of reflection and action in the Western Church. The very number of liturgical actions that can be referred to as sacraments was only set at seven – a mystical number in the Jewish and Christian traditions – in the Middle Ages, each one justified by reference to words or actions of Jesus. This is the tradition we inherit. Let us begin, then, with a brief overview of that inheritance.

In the liturgy of Baptism, candidates are cleansed of original sin and become part of the Christian community, the body of Christ, deemed worthy to participate in the sacred meal of the Eucharist. In confirmation, through the action of anointing with oil, the Spirit of God is conferred upon a new or maturing Christian.

In the Eucharist itself, the community prepares itself, through hearing and meditating on the word of God, to witness the re-presentation of the sacrifice of Calvary at the hands of the priest, as the body and blood of the risen and glorified Christ become present on the altar under the form of bread and wine; it prepares, too, to participate in the sacred meal of that body and blood which unites the human community with God in a life-giving communion.

139

In confession or reconciliation, members of the community who have failed to live according to the expectations of the community and of God are reconciled to God and their fellow Christians. In the sacrament of the sick, oil and the prayer of a presbyter bring comfort and healing to those who are ill or dying.

In the sacrament of marriage the union of a Christian man and woman is strengthened by and becomes a representation of the loving action of God in Christ. In the sacrament of ordination, ministers are chosen for the church and receive the gifts of the Spirit, the authority and the power they need to carry out their duties, whether as deacon, priest or bishop.

All of these practices have evolved through time with the passage of Western Christianity through different cultural and ideological milieux. They are the principal points of encounter between the ministers of the Church and the ordinary worshippers, and they provide the primary context for teaching and communal celebration. Within a practising Catholic perspective they have the transparency and comfort of familiarity, yet from without they can appear arbitrary when compared with parallel developments in other Christian traditions and with the New Testament world in which they claim to be rooted. The particular dilemma for modern people is that it seems difficult to avoid reading them either as a sort of magic in which God's gracious action appears to be presumed, or as a communal expression of faith which has neither more nor less value than a family get-together. Finally the historical development of a priestly caste and of a barrier between clergy and laity which conditions the form of these liturgical celebrations seem both far removed from the more fluid community structures implied in the New Testament and poorly adapted to a democratised, post-enlightenment culture.

A part of the answer has already been stated: God communicates to us in the language that we can understand. Any given language, including the language and practice of collective worship, will be the product of a history and a culture. In some sense the forms of words and action or community structures that enable communication to take place in any given era will be arbitrary. Accordingly we can accept the forms and assumptions of Catholic sacramental practice as long as they continue to communicate to Christians the power and the love of God. Difficulties only arise when people find themselves alienated from those practices, perhaps as a result of intellectual difficulties or perhaps because of conflicting cultural assumptions.

For instance, if I cannot see that I have done anything wrong or cannot see the point of telling a priest about what I have done wrong, then I will find little reason to go to confession. Again, if I cannot make sense of 'transubstantiation' or find the language of sacrifice disturbing, then I will be uncomfortable with the Christian celebration *par excellence*, the Eucharist. If I do not see that love requires a lifetime's commitment, then I will not enter Christian marriage. When I see little evidence of healing as a result of administering the sacrament of the sick, I will question its purpose, and perhaps, by analogy, the purpose of all the sacraments. When I fail to observe noticeable strength, power, joy in the Spirit in those who receive the sacraments of confirmation and

141

ordination (why is not every bishop, priest and confirmation candidate an inspirational preacher?) I may likewise question the real purpose of these actions. Painfully, if I have been judged unworthy to participate in the life of the Christian community on grounds with which I happen to disagree, then its sacraments and its ministers become an object of distrust. More painfully still, when I see those who participate in and organise the sacramental life of the community acting unworthily, my faith in the whole structure is called into question.

But if the sacraments are not magic rituals and yet are a vital part of Christian life, then it is for two reasons. Firstly, because they are an expression of the faith of the people of God that God fulfils her promises and secondly, because this faith invites God's loyal response of gracious action and always receives it, not because of a mechanism, nor because of a compulsion, but because that is how God is. This sacred transaction is independent of the state of belief or the quality of life of any one participant or minister within the believing community. That is the justification of the medieval expression 'ex opere operato', that sacraments are accomplished 'through their performance'. This only makes sense when we understand that the performance takes place in the wider context of the faithful life of the community of God.

But if this is so, if sacraments are moments in which the community can encounter the gracious action of God, then we need to be helped when we struggle to find faith in those moments. This might mean developing an understanding of 'sacrament' that we can find intellectually more coherent. Or it might mean finding liturgical forms which allow us to express our faith transparently, without inner reservations. It might also mean reconciling our own understanding of the Christian way with the rhetoric of the institutional Church. I want to focus here on the first two (the last will be deferred to a later chapter). I will begin with some general remarks about sacraments and then concentrate on the Eucharist or Mass, because that is the principal place where the majority of Catholic Christians meet to worship as a community.

Sacrament and mysteries: a history of meaning.

In a phrase from the council of Trent (quoted in the modern Catechism) sacraments 'confer the grace they signify'. That council speaks in the same sentence of the sacraments 'containing' the grace they signify. On the one hand, a gracious action of God for his community takes place through the performance by the community of a ritual act. On the other, the ritual itself shows us symbolically the nature of God's gracious action. This definition relates to an earlier definition of Augustine (5th Century), who speaks of the rituals of the Old Testament as 'a visible sacrifice, the sacrament (that is, the sacred sign) of the invisible sacrifice'. The ritual action is symbolic and points beyond itself to the reality which is hidden in God. Notice, however, that the definition of Trent has moved away from the model of a sign numerically distinct from the thing signed, though participating in it, to a definition in which the sign 'contains' the signed.

This development probably reflects the intense focus in the Western church, from the 10th Century onwards, on the theology and

143

spirituality of the Eucharist; above all the emergence of a strong theology of the real presence of Christ in the bread and wine and a corresponding development in cultic practice. I would suggest that the way of thinking which refers to *all* sacraments as holy things *containing* grace, rather than as holy *signs of* or *pathways to* ultimate reality arises out of a concern to make specific sense of the body of Christ as the sacrament *par excellence*, in which an *identity* is claimed to exist between the one object that appears as bread and the one body of Christ which it represents.

I will return to the topic of the real presence a little later, but first I want to look at older understandings of the word 'sacrament', which are also a part of the tradition and which I believe offer wider scope for understanding in the modern context than the definition with which we started. Here, I am to some extent rehearsing thought which is a standard part of 20th Century theology, and is present in most modern expositions of the sacraments, including that of the Catechism.

It is important to recall that our description of sacraments as containing and conferring the grace they signify stems from the Middle Ages. However, in antiquity, the Latin word 'sacramentum' was not used with anything like this sense. It comes into the Latin Christian lexicon as a translation of the Greek word 'mysterion' (frequently used in the New Testament) which we more often translate as 'mystery'. This word takes us into the wider religious culture of the ancient world, in which secret rituals were celebrated to different gods (Cybele, Isis, Mithras), including rites of purgation and mystical rebirth. The plural 'mysteries' denotes the rituals themselves, the singular, the saving truth hidden from all but the initiates. Because the New Testament writers make use of this word, its Latin translators must look for an equivalent.

It is, then, a little surprising that the primary meaning of the Latin 'sacramentum' is 'oath'. The reason it came to be used as a translation of 'mysterion' and to refer to the rituals of Baptism and Eucharist is, perhaps, that mystery religions often do seem to have included an oath – if only an oath not to divulge the secrets to the uninitiated. Correspondingly, Christians, in the course of Baptism, made promises which they renewed in the Eucharist. Evidence from the second century (Pliny the Younger) suggests that Christians used to make a 'sacramentum' (oath) to keep the Ten Commandments at their weekly meetings and shared meal. Perhaps, too, the word captures something of the notion of Covenant, which is presented in Christ and expressed and renewed through Baptism and Eucharist. All this being so, we are entitled by the tradition to use the Greek 'mysterion' (secret) or 'mysteria' (plural = mystery cult) as a helpful tool for rethinking sacraments. We need, however, to take a closer look at why the language of mystery religions might have been attractive to Christians.

The mystery religions of the ancient world seem to have consisted in the re-enactment of sacred dramas of rebirth, centring on myths about the tutelary deity. These re-enactments were a means which allowed the witnesses, prepared by an initiation that freed them from guilt, to participate in the realities (the heavenly rebirth) which the mysteries represented. It seems no accident that New Testament writers choose to talk about the mystery or mysteries of Christ as they proclaim the Gospel in their own time. For them Christ's are the real,

145

saving actions of death and resurrection, in which his followers participate through the rite of initiation (in Baptism we die with Christ) and participation (whenever you eat this bread and drink the cup, you proclaim the death of the Lord). The later forms of Christian worship seem to have modelled themselves expressly on the generally attractive model of the mystery religions, so that by the fifth Century, presence at the central part of the Eucharist is open only to the fully initiated (the baptised). Those who await baptism (the Catechumens) are dismissed before that part of the ritual begins. The liturgy is shaped to inspire awe in the presence of the Holy. In this early example of inculturation (adaptation to the culture of the time) the Christian Eucharist becomes a moving icon (image, reflection) of the heavenly mysteries, the saving action of God through Christ, which is timelessly valid. Those who participate in the liturgy also participate in the realities to which they refer.

If this is the foundational meaning of 'sacrament', then for Christians 'sacrament' is indeed, as Augustine says, a sacred sign of the mysterious saving action of Christ. Christ himself in his saving action is the foundational mystery of which the sacred signs are echoes. With such an understanding, Karl Rahner can suggest that the Church itself is a sacrament, as the *community* which is a sacred sign of God's saving action in the world. But in another sense, as we can see, there are two 'model' sacraments in which that community encounters the reality of its own redemption and salvation: Baptism (initiation) and Eucharist (participation). Those other things which we call sacraments are so only in a derivative sense. They are sacraments insofar as they imply

146

participation in some aspect of the mystery of Christ's death and resurrection. But in this derivative sense, there will be many more events, inside and outside the context of liturgy, which will be sacramental for Christian believers. These will be moments when the Spirit engages with and enlivens the believer through the medium of shared experience. They will be moments of communication, strengthening of love and understanding, signs that the love of God poured out for them in Jesus the Lord is not just words, but something real, consoling, enabling and present.

The Eucharist as sacrifice

What, then, do the text and action of the Eucharist signify? In the central part of the celebration, they *refer to* specific moments in the narrative of the saving action of Jesus: the anamnesis (recalling) of the last supper, death, resurrection, present union, gift of the Spirit, future coming. Characteristically the liturgical texts that we use make this reference *through a narrative* of sacrifice. 'See the victim whose death has reconciled us to yourself'. Such language is common to the Eucharistic prayers of East and West, reaching back into antiquity. But that language already implies that in the Eucharist, the sacrifice of Christ is, at least symbolically, re-enacted. In the dominant theology of the Middle Ages, an understanding developed that the sacrifice of Christ is 're-presented' in the Mass. This understanding was canonised in the council of Trent in response to the critique of the reformers, and is reaffirmed in the modern Catechism.

The language of sacrifice itself is not easy for modern ears, and in the next chapter we shall take some time to explore ways of understanding and rereading that language. For now I want to look at a more basic paradox thrown up by that language when we look at different things that Christians have said about sacrifice, about the sacrifice of Christ and about their Eucharist through the centuries.

The Letter to the Hebrews in the New Testament presents an elaborate and sensitive argument to a Jewish audience, which both affirms their traditional belief in and love of the Law and the practice of sacrifice, and leads them to the point at which they can take their leave of them, because in Christ the purpose of those sacrifices has been fulfilled. A possible audience may be educated Jewish Christians from the Diaspora, who are struggling to come to terms with the destruction of the Temple in Jerusalem. At any rate, the author of Hebrews wishes to make clear the importance and value of the tradition that is superseded by the saving action of Jesus Christ.

The author makes use of the concept that the elements of the Jewish ritual stand in the relationship of earthly sign to heavenly mystery. He did not invent this style of reading the tradition: other Jewish writers (Philo, Josephus) and other New Testament writers (Paul, John) make similar moves. This particular way of reading text and practice as an allegory for a higher truth, or a higher reality, is generally referred to as 'typology'. In echoes of Platonic thought (think of the relationship of the world of the forms, the super-realities, to the world of the senses), events and characters in Old Testament history and forms of Jewish practice become 'types' (images or

148

foreshadowings) of realities which are made present in the history of Jesus Christ. We can note again how Augustine actually labels these visible sacrifices 'sacraments' as 'a holy sign of the invisible (sacrifice)'. The earthly 'type', rooted in human experience and history, offers us the beginnings of an explanation of the reality to which it refers, but is then eclipsed by that reality.

For this reason, the Letter to the Hebrews offers us a detailed account of the nature of sacrifice. For instance, in Heb. 9, 11 – 14, we read that the traditional blood sacrifices cleanse from physical pollutions – those arising from contact with the dead or with the flow of bodily fluids – but Christ's sacrifice cleanses 'our conscience from dead actions, so that we can serve the living God'. There follows an argument that to establish the new covenant, a death was necessary (as was the case with the old covenant, Exodus 24, 6). The covenant is not secure, does not have force without the death of the covenanter (here interpreted as 'testator'). In other words, the inheritance cannot be shared out until the person who made the will is dead. The author adds (9, 22) the general observation that just about everything is cleansed by blood and that without blood there is no release.

One way or another, for this writer, bloodshed and sacrifice represent a part of the order of things, a mechanism which is effective. There is a science of sacrifice. He needs to affirm this efficacy if the language of sacrifice is to provide a real explanation for what Christ does. And yet the thrust of his argument is that, in reality, those ancient sacrifices only pointed the way and now, with the advent of Christ, their purpose has come to an end. There is no more sacrifice. He climbs the ladder of typology only to throw it away when he gets to the top.

The logical conclusion is that there is no further need for sacrifice. Indeed, the way the Christians presented themselves in the first centuries and the way they were understood in the wider culture was as people who did not sacrifice to the gods. While the Temple stood, and while Christians could enjoy the protection of the synagogues, they could get by without joining in the local sacrifices on behalf of the Emperor – sacrifices were offered in the Jerusalem Temple on Caesar's behalf. But without the Temple sacrifice and without synagogue protection, Christians were exposed as people who would neither join in the local sacrifices nor sacrifice according to a cult of their own. This became an element in their persecution. In the anonymous 'Letter to Diognetus', in which an early 2nd Century Christian tries to justify the faith and practice of Christianity, the author affirms the absurdity of sacrificing to the almighty God, whether as the pagans do or according to the Jewish Law. The implication is that Christians do not understand themselves as offering sacrifices.

However, in another 2nd Century letter (the first letter of Clement to the Corinthians) we find instructions for preserving the due order in worship; we find priests and bishops compared to the high priest and the priests of the old covenant. We find the language of oblation and offering. From here we can trace a reverse typology, which echoes throughout the history of the Church, in which the structures of the Old Testament worshipping community not only prefigure, but also suggest determinations for the structures of the

Christian communities. With this comes, in spite of what the Letter to Diognetus claims, a reaffirmation of the language of offering and sacrifice. At the end of the 2nd century, Irenaeus of Lyons will declare that sacrifice and offerings continue under the New Law as under the Old. Irenaeus was keen to emphasise the continuity between the Old Testament and the New, and of course the language of sacrifice is integral to both.

Yet even so, the use of that language is not as simple as it looks. Already Old Testament texts allegorise sacrifice: true sacrifice is accomplished through right action and right disposition. 'My sacrifice a contrite spirit, a humbled contrite heart you will not spurn' says the singer in Psalm 50. Psalm 40 (quoted in Hebrews) 'You wanted not sacrifice or cereal offering, but you gave me an open ear.' One can point also to the relativising of cultic activity by the prophets (Amos, Hosea, Isaiah, Jeremiah) in the face of collective injustice. So we can find New Testament readings like those of Paul (Romans 12,1), who can call on Christians to present *their bodies* as a living sacrifice, and of the first letter of Peter (2, 5), where the community is encouraged to become a living temple in which spiritual sacrifices, pleasing to the Lord are offered. The sacrifice of Christians is the witness of their lives, conformed to Christ.

So when, in the early centuries, Christian worship is spoken of as a sacrifice, it is as a sacrifice of praise (hence the term 'Eucharist', from the Greek word for thanksgiving), and the primary reference of 'sacrifice' is to the action of the community living out its vocation. This is the interpretation of Christian sacrifice, for instance, which

151

Augustine presents in his 'City of God' (5th Century). Augustine rehearses arguments similar to those of the letter to Diognetus to assert the pointlessness of sacrificial ritual. He differs from the earlier letter in that he affirms the value of the visible Jewish sacrifices as 'sacramenta' (sacred signs) of the invisible sacrifice. But when he talks about the sacrifice of Christians, he states that the true sacrifices of Christians are their works of mercy towards their neighbours and towards themselves. The essence of Christian sacrifice is the identity of Christians with the body of Christ, who sacrifices himself. This sacrifice is celebrated in sacred sign (sacrament) in the liturgy, where those assembled witness that they themselves are being offered in the offering.

We can begin to see how, out of antiquity the liturgy of the Eucharist provides a symbolic representation of two sacrifices: the present sacrifice of the people of God, carried out through the faithful living of their Christian lives, and the eternal sacrifice of Jesus, with whom they are united. This is not yet the Medieval Mass, as a re-presentation of the eternal sacrifice of Jesus. For that, the Western Church must engage with other cultures and discover a new need for cultic, sacrificial action, which it will justify (by typology) with reference to the cult of the Old Testament. There will always be dissent from this majority position, boiling over into the conflicts of the Reformation. But the council of Trent will affirm the identity of Christ's sacrifice and the Mass, and include in its justification the anthropological claim that human nature requires a visible sacrifice (a claim quoted in the modern Catechism).

The modern liturgy does much to recover the powerful idea of the symbolic self-offering of the community and other aspects of the liturgy of the early Church, though our heritage, viewed over the centuries, leaves us with some unresolved contradictions. Nevertheless, we also have some powerful ideas, which can help us understand what we do through the Eucharist in the modern world. If the Mass is a representation of the self-offering of the community, united with the self-offering of Christ, then it acquires a new power in contexts where Christians are themselves suffering, being persecuted and killed. Liberation theology has given the Church a new insight into the identity of Christ with the suffering poor. The liturgy becomes a sacred sign of a reality lived out in a history that is not yet fully redeemed. Equally, although we may be ambivalent about a literal understanding of the language of sacrifice, if we understand the Eucharist as a sacred sign of the reality of Christ's action for us, referred to *through* the metaphor of sacrifice, then we can begin to make sense of that other challenging concept in the theology of the Eucharist: the real presence. To this let us now turn.

The Real Presence and sacred drama

The language given to the Christian community by Jesus, 'This is my body, this is my blood' has been controversial from its earliest times, as is clear from the dialogues of chapter 6 of John's Gospel, which ends with a group of Jesus' disciples walking away. The fact that different Christian writers take the trouble to expound the meaning of the words in different places and different centuries is an indication that they have been a continual source of debate. But, as with the language of sacrifice just discussed, the words used do not always mean quite what they first seem to.

When we look at 2nd Century texts, we find, as before, more than one way of talking about the Eucharist. In the Didache, a short text which claims to represent the teaching of the apostles, there are instructions for those leading the Eucharist. In the instructions on the Eucharist, the prayer over the wine refers to it as a symbol of Jesus, and the prayer over the bread refers to it as a symbol of the life and knowledge brought by Jesus (a reading implied in John 6 as well). The bread itself is a symbol of the unity of the Church and the meal is 'spiritual nourishment'.

Other writers, close in time (Ignatius, Irenaeus) will be more specific in interpreting the words of Jesus from the Last Supper as a true statement – albeit without exploring any conceptual problems this might raise, though Irenaeus does talk of an earthly element and a heavenly element joined in the Eucharist. Some authors (Cyril of Jerusalem, Gregory of Nyssa) ask their readers to believe that the bread is the Lord's body because that is what he, the Lord, has said. Yet all the while, it must be remembered, the practice of the Eucharist is being presented as a part of an integrated Christian life, in which the community themselves represent the real presence of the body of Christ. So Augustine, addressing those who are about to be baptised and witness the sacred mysteries for the first time, can tell them to think of themselves, as body of Christ, being offered in the liturgy.

Elsewhere, the literalism of 'eat my body' is mitigated by Cyril (4th Century) with the qualification 'in figure' (= 'type') – which takes us back to the familiar relationship of 'type' and 'reality'.

So the idea that the body and blood of Christ are present in the Eucharist was affirmed from early on in the Christian communities. But there were a number of ways available for making sense of this – or at least there were until the 11th Century, when Berengar of Tours was challenged for claiming that the bread and wine were only a 'sacramentum' (sacred sign) and not the real body and blood of Christ. Berengar was obliged to make a retraction and out of the dispute was born the distinctive Western Medieval theology of a *substantial* identity between the bread and wine and the glorified body and blood of Christ. In 1215 the term 'transubstantiation' was first used in an official document, the word being adapted from the newly recovered philosophy science of Aristotle. It was not the only term used to try and state philosophically what had become an integral part of personal and communal devotional life, but it was the one that was eventually confirmed by Trent and which is preserved in our Catechism.

For moderns, the least of our problems is that the Aristotelian language is not our way of talking about reality. Thomas Aquinas himself acknowledged that the concept of transubstantiation violated even Aristotle's rules. According to those rules the appearance of an object – comprising its 'accidental' properties – is supposed to vary with any change in its nature. Yet in transubstantiation there is a change of nature without a change in appearance. Here too, as we have seen before, a standard language breaks when pushed to its limits. But

155

we, with our understanding of an essential link between the matter of which an object consists and the appearance it presents to our senses, struggle to make headway with the strong identity claim that that which in every respect appears to be bread is identical with the risen body of the Lord.

Curiously enough, we can be helped by the medieval theologians, because they were prepared to think things through to the end. So we find that, by affirming the identity, a number of paradoxes are generated: the whole Christ is received in any one fragment of host and in any drop from the wine; yet Christ is not multiplied by being present in many fragments or drops, nor is he diminished by being consumed. When we recognise this, we realise that the language of identity is itself broken. If the identity statement is true, it is unlike any other identity that we can know and we are therefore entitled to search for other ways of appropriating the claim from the tradition that the flesh and blood of Christ are present in the bread and in the wine .

If a literal reading of the traditional language does not work, then we are perhaps being invited to search, in the tradition of Origen, for a 'spiritual' reading of this theological text. We affirm that Christ is present as victim and redeemer in the Eucharist. We accept that he nourishes us with the life won by him, through his sacrifice, in the sacred meal we share. We can translate some of this into the language that we developed earlier, using boundary metaphysics. We could talk about the inexhaustible energy of Christ, shaped in God-time, being transferred into or breaking into our own time. And this energy is more than mere joules: it is the Spirit of love, which transforms the whole person, body and soul. It is a reality that enters the physical world by transforming the person of the worshipper. Using this sort of language we can begin to make sense of 'my flesh is real food'.

But by making this step, we have already moved back into another mode of conceiving of the Eucharist, the mode we used when we conceived of it as sacrifice. There, our focus was not so much on a single object (the bread), as the action of the liturgy; and the reference of that action was not to an object (the glorified body of Christ) but to an event, described as sacrifice, the saving action of Christ. Our attention to the objects, bread and wine, has distracted us from the nature of the Eucharist as action – as life, rather than a still life.

The Eucharist is celebrated by people who speak, act and pray in time. By entering into the action of these words and these movements, they enter a space in which the saving action of God, Father, Son and Spirit, becomes accessible. Rather than God coming down into our world, we step into God's world, where the saving actions of Christ – from the proclamation of the Kingdom to his last meal with his disciples and his death on the cross, together with his final victory over sin and death – are all timelessly present. Our actions in the Eucharist are bound to the reality of Christ who does this for us. Because the Word became flesh, the Son of God remains eternally entangled with our physical and time-bound world. When we enter the space of the Eucharist, we, whose actions and prayers take place in time, resonate with the timeless reality which shapes our lives. As we offer the bread, break it and share it, he is really present as the one who saves us and gives us life; and if we did not offer the bread, he would

157

not be present in this way. We are nourished as we eat the host and, if we did not eat the host, we would not receive the deeper nourishment which he offers in this space and through this action.

The Eucharist becomes again a mystery-ritual, a liturgical action creating a space in which we can encounter Christ as the one who saves us. Through that encounter, our lives and our witness are strengthened. It is the encounter with Christ that allows us to call the other official rituals 'sacraments' as well. And by this definition there are many more sacraments, moments in our lives in which the love of God becomes incarnate in our history, in which the greater narrative of our lives becomes palpable. Whenever in a life-changing moment we encounter the one who saves us, we enter the mystery once more.

The lived reality

But there is a real barrier to our understanding of the Eucharist in the gulf between what it claims to be about (the cosmic mystery of our redemption in Christ) and what we experience – sitting in a room full of people we hardly know, occasionally joining in the recitation of a form of words and sometimes struggling to stay focused on the things we are supposed to be thinking about. It is not often that weekly Mass, the focal point of meeting and worship of the Christian community, is a dynamic religious experience for the majority of the participants. There is a gap between the worthy, sometimes, dull, sometimes enjoyable, sometimes uplifting liturgies which we experience (or lead) week in week out and the power and energy that seem to have been present in the first Christian communities as described to us by Paul and Luke.

The revolution in Roman Catholic practice of the Mass since the second Vatican Council has been fruitful, but in some ways the resultant text ended up being neither one thing nor the other. The old text of Trent, adapted from antiquity, was a treasury rich in biblical reference for those who could follow, while the action and even the vestments were (as in the days of the High Priest in Jerusalem) rich in symbolism. This was indeed a descendant of the 'mystery religion' model of Eucharist. The initiate sees, watches, hears, and is drawn into contemplation of the higher world of which the sacred action is a mere representation. The principle can be seen clearly in Orthodox worship, where the participant is given the freedom to stay, move, light candles, pray, chant in the sacred space created by the liturgy. Importantly, you are not obliged to think about everything that is going on, nor to understand everything that is going on, you are merely invited to find God in the midst of this space, these words, this action.

The principle that the text of the liturgy should be accessible to worshippers is a good one – especially in the matter of scripture readings. In theory, it gives the community an opportunity to engage much more directly with the liturgy. Unfortunately what has been produced is a text so complex and wordy that Mass can often become a demanding exercise in passive listening, rather than an opportunity to find echoes of the mystery of Christ. Because the text is in a language that is understood, the participants can feel obliged to attend to the

159

whole (or else they have not been to Mass properly). Their freedom to pray and contemplate is thus impeded by the text itself.

There are two directions one could take at this point with the Eucharist, both differently advantageous. One would be to produce a minimalist text of the Mass, designed for the more immediate engagement of the people, and which invites them to a greater participatory role than is at present available to them. Active listening and exchange engages people much better than passive listening. The other is to return to the old version (or to develop a modern alternative) of the traditional liturgy, which would allow people to rediscover a sense of contemplation in the liturgy.

The first direction leads towards something closer to the early Christian communities described by Paul, and might enable Catholic communities to rediscover a more powerful sense of Christ-present-in-the-community and the power of the Spirit, through the encouragement of wider active participation by community members other than the priest. The second direction could lead us towards a shared experience of cosmic mystery through liturgy.

But perhaps the root of the problem is less in the form of the Mass, than in the fact that the weekly Mass is often isolated as the only experience of Christian community and the only significant experience of prayer during the week. Yet in an ideal world the Eucharist should be an expression of the commitment of community members to a faith that extends beyond the confines of the hour in Church on a Sunday. The Eucharist will take on depth and richness when we who participate in it are engaged actively with our fellow Christians as a real community, reflecting on our faith, working out our salvation and searching for the will of God in our lives. To enter fully into the liturgy of the Eucharist, we need to become the sacrifice.

Chapter 11   Sacrifice and Salvation

As we have seen, Roman Catholicism, through its liturgy, through the long theological tradition and through the sacred texts of the Old and New Testament, is committed to the language of sacrifice. The New Testament writers first use this language to explain what it is that Jesus does for us and how his death brings us salvation. The sacrifices of the Old Testament are signs that explain the action of Jesus, whose death on the cross is thus a sacrifice that takes away our sins and rescues us from death. It is prefigured in the sacrifices on the Day of Atonement and in the Passover lamb, whose blood causes the angel of death to pass by. This sacrifice is then re-presented in the Eucharist, around which the Roman Catholic priesthood is defined.

There is, as has been suggested, an inbuilt paradox in the continued Christian use of this language. We can sharpen it in this way: the sacrifice of Christ accomplishes in reality what the sacrifice of animals claims to do but cannot. That is, the practice of animal sacrifice for purification and reparation of sins is, in the end, only there to provide a metaphor for what Christ accomplishes by his suffering and death (Augustine's 'sacrament'). But if the practice is not doing anything real, how can it provide a basis for explaining what Christ accomplishes?

The answer lies, as we have seen, in the ancient tradition of allegorical reading taken up in the letter to the Hebrews. True sacrifice is not accomplished in cultic action but by carrying out the will of God in obedience. What is offered up is Christ's will, to the will of the

162

Father. The act of obedience is metaphorically a sacrifice, the absolute gift of something precious and irreplaceable to God. When Thomas Aquinas asks whether it is appropriate to speak of Christ's action as sacrifice he begins by quoting Augustine: 'true sacrifice is every work that is performed so that we may cleave to God in holy fellowship'. Thomas then suggests that because the work of Christ in which he, of his own free will, endured suffering was acceptable to God (since it was inspired by love [for humanity]), it is appropriate to say that he offered himself in suffering for us.

If it is doing the will of the Father that makes the difference, then we can accept the use of the language of sacrifice as part of the tradition familiar from our sacred texts, as a metaphor. But where the metaphor has lost its roots in a practice, as is the case in the western world, it ceases to explain – no matter how comprehensible it is. So if we are to ask ourselves the deeper question about what difference the obedience of Christ or his physical death have made, we need to look for another language that will offer us a way to deeper understanding.

A key term is the phrase 'for us', which goes back to (probably) the earliest surviving synopsis of Christian belief (1 Corinthians 15), as used in catechesis. It has its roots in the early Christian reading of Isaiah 53: 'he was being wounded for our rebellions, crushed because of our guilt'. The term can be understood easily in the context of sacrifice, in which the (animal) victim substitutes for someone else. So in the sacrifice for the first born reported in Luke 2, the animal substitutes for the new-born child, who is 'owed' to God. In Leviticus 16, on the Day of Atonement, the scapegoat is chosen to carry the sins of the people out into the desert. The familiar patterns of sacrifice provide a rich system of analogy for the action of Christ, and the sacrificial 'explanation' of 'for us' also finds roots in Isaiah 53: 'He gave his life as a sin-offering'. For our understanding, however, it is more useful, initially, to read the term in a forensic frame of reference.

Judgment and justification

One of the most significant theological genealogies in Western Christianity is the line from Paul (above all, in the letter to the Romans) and through Augustine to Martin Luther. Augustine rereads Paul, and Luther rereads Paul and Augustine in order to explain, in different contexts, that Christ brings justification to humanity. I will not rehearse anything of these developments here. I merely want to point out how important the language of justification has been in Western Christianity as a way of thinking about salvation, and then to search for ways in which this, and associated language, might still provide understanding for us today. I will talk about Paul's specific agenda with regard to the Jewish Law in more detail in a later chapter. Here I want to pick out from the letter to the Romans two different background narratives that are used to explain what it is we are being rescued from and to look at what might be meant by the concept of 'justice' or 'righteousness'.

The first narrative (Romans 1 – 2) is a version of the fall of humanity borrowed from the wider Hellenistic Jewish culture; a similar example can be found in the book of Wisdom, from the 1st Century BCE. The narrative is clearly designed to challenge a contemporary gentile audience: humanity could have known God through the contemplation of the universe, but deliberately chose not to recognise the author of all things, preferring to worship created things and the work of their hands; because of this, God 'handed them over' to the cravings of their hearts, leading to uncleanness, 'unnatural' sexual practices and then to all sorts of injustice, wickedness, greed, evil, jealousy, murder, strife and treachery. The charge against them reads that, although they know the just judgment of God – that all who do such things are worthy of death – they continue to do them and encourage others to do so. They are, therefore, fully culpable. Because of this, no-one is in a position to judge anyone, and no-one is exempt from judgment, even if this is deferred by the mercy of God (who gives time for repentance) to the last day, the 'day of wrath'.

The second narrative (Romans 5) is rooted in the story of Adam, as the first human being. Through one man sin entered the world, and through sin death, and so death passed to all people in that all sinned. Unfortunately Paul's text becomes ambiguous at this point, but what he wants to do is lay the foundations for an explanatory analogy: 'For if, by the transgression of one man, the many died, so much the more did the grace of God and the free gift in the gracious action of the one man, Jesus Christ, abound for the many'. Here the source of sin and death needs to be the one man who is at the source of all humanity, so that we can begin to understand how in one man, Jesus Christ, we can be saved from those things. It is this narrative that leads Augustine (with his literal reading of Genesis) to formulate the doctrine of original sin; and it is this narrative that leads the modern Church, even though it

165

broadly accepts evolutionary theory, to resist a 'many ancestors' theory of the origin of humanity.

For us, because we cannot read Genesis as more than a parable, the first narrative is more helpful. Like the parable of Genesis, though purporting to give a history of a process of degradation, it is much better read as a timeless statement about the present. The breakdown in the relationship with God entails a breakdown in our relationship with the world, with ourselves and with one another. As we all participate in this broken situation, we are all sinners. Because we are sinners (according to Paul) we are both liable to judgment and unable to escape it, except by the mercy of God.

Paul's understanding of sin (we have all sinned and fallen short of the glory of God) as a fact of life for a weakened humanity that is constantly dependent on the grace of God is similar to that found in the writings of the contemporary Jewish sect in Qumran, but probably different from that of the Pharisees, who endeavour to live righteously (in justice before God) by faithfully fulfilling the commandments of the Law. Paul is making a theological option within the terms of Jewish thought. For him this approach is a necessary step if he is to show that Christ is the one in whom that which we cannot do is accomplished.

So all people are liable to judgment on the 'day of wrath' because they have failed to recognise God, and, as a result, have sinned, have failed to represent the glory of God in their lives. They are unjust in two senses. First, they have done wrong and need to pay the penalty if they are to be at rights with God. Second, of themselves they cannot become *'just' people*, that is: people who are virtuous, with the inner

166

strength and disposition to produce good actions. And they are not in a position to do anything about either their juridical or their moral state without turning to God. Because of their juridical state, they deserve death but, by the grace of God, Christ dies for them. This frees them from the juridical penalty and renders them legally just before God, reconciled. Then by the new life of the resurrection, they receive the Spirit of God, which enables them to live the new life as people who possess the virtue of justice.

Later theologians will endeavour to tease out how it is that Christ can pay on our behalf the penalty we owe. Paul, as we have seen, hints that he is a second Adam, the first-born of a new creation. Athanasius, the father of the Nicene Creed will argue in the 4th century that the nature of the debt is such that only someone who is both God and man could repay it. That line of argument is developed, too, by Anselm of Canterbury in the 11th Century, in his treatise 'Why did God become human?' The debt owed to God is so great that only God could pay it; yet because it is owed by humanity, it must be paid by a human being.

We can understand this narrative of the courtroom, since it is a part of the reality we experience and does offer a real explanation of the meaning of 'for us'. In a human courtroom, however, the procedures and the penalties are the result of human choice and people do not have to die when they have committed a crime: the lawmakers can decree other penalties. Equally, if the lawmakers want to forgive someone, it is possible to issue a pardon and there is no absolute necessity for reparation. Could not God do likewise?

There are a number of different ways of imagining God's relation to court procedures. One (Rev. 12,12, see also, John 12,31) gives a leading role to the devil, who stands before the throne of God, accusing our brothers and sisters night and day; but, 'they conquered him because of the blood of the lamb and the word of their testimony'. The implication here is that the rules of court are not entirely in God's hands: there is a mechanism to which God is subordinate, which is represented by the person of the accuser referred to in John as 'the ruler of this world'.

For Augustine, the judgment and the penalty are presented as an inevitable consequence of God's justice. The logic of absolute justice demands both that all human beings be found guilty *and* that they receive the due penalty of death. Anselm, too, argues from first principles that humanity, for its disobedience, owes an unpayable burden of debt. So the court of law and its rules are part of the logical consequence of the world chosen by God in which human beings freely disobey her. God is bound by logical necessity. If they want to save humanity, the Son must identify with and substitute for humanity in a court which is God's own.

We could, on the other hand, protect God's freedom and suppose that she freely chooses to deal with human sin through the mechanism of judgment and punishment, even though there might have been other ways of dealing with it. But this is problematic. We acknowledge God's freedom to do what she wills but at the price of bewilderment, that she should *choose* a means of salvation in which the beloved Son suffers and dies.

168

So while the courtroom model does provide a context that makes sense of the 'for us' of scripture, it also leaves us with deeper and more disturbing questions about God's love and justice. If our human justice no longer seeks to kill people for what they have done, why should the justice of an absolutely loving God be harsher than our own?

An alternative is to move out of the courtroom and return to the idea of a mechanism that the Son of God engages with in order to overthrow it. This explanation, too, can be drawn from the New Testament (again, John 12, 31, Mk 3, 22). We are familiar with the idea of emergent structures, physical, psychological, social, economic in our picture of the evolution of the world in freedom. The parable of Adam and Eve and the Salvation History of the Old Testament suggest that, at any one time, the world is both growing away from and growing towards God. So we can make sense of the idea that in a world in constant, free dialogue with God, powerful structures emerge that affect all levels of human life, and that some of these are malign. Such mechanisms might have the character of a hostile and powerful intelligence, something like the figure that John denotes by the term 'ruler of this world' (the invisible hand of the world markets). These mechanisms present a real barrier to humanity's ability to live in the presence of God, but because they are emergent structures in the universe, they can only be broken from within. Thus God freely chooses to subordinate his Son to an alien juridical structure for the sake of humanity. Entering the world, Jesus plays the game according to the rules that have evolved there. By dying, he endures the force of those rules in solidarity with humanity and, by rising and inaugurating the new creation, he opens a pathway for humanity to a new way of living in our time which binds us to a mysterious fullness of life in eternity.

There is more than one theology which has explored this line of thought. Liberation theology has identified structural injustice as a mechanism from which suffering humanity needs to be liberated, and developed a compelling way of reading and living Christian text. In particular it has highlighted the liberating role of the life and preaching of Jesus in any account of salvation. Salvation and liberation take place in a whole history of which the death and resurrection are a part. But here I want to focus on a theory which identifies another sort of structure, and which unites the language of the courtroom and the language of sacrifice.

The Scapegoat Theory of Girard

So far, we have primarily thought of the system of sacrifice as something that God might want. But it is also possible to conceive of it as the product of sinful structures, progressively refined and purified by God. In this we acknowledge the dark side of sacrifice, the human sacrifices and the search for a victim, echoes of which are found in the explicit prophetic rejection of sacrifices to Moloch and the substitute of the ram for Isaac in Genesis 18. The thinker René Girard, observing this phenomenon, has developed an anthropological theory of a mechanism embedded in human group-psychology that conceals itself in social structures that identify and destroy victims. Theologians like Raymund Schwager have made use of Girard's ideas to read the life, death and resurrection of Jesus as a narrative about the confrontation and ultimate overthrow of this dehumanising mechanism.

A crude version of the theory runs something like this: human beings are imitative and learn from one another to desire things (think of modern advertising methods). Because of this, human beings in any group will find themselves in competition for the same things. This leads to conflict within the group, which, if allowed to go unchecked, will tear it apart. Over time, the group (human society) develops a juridical and cultic structure that allows the collective violence to be directed against a chosen victim (or victims). The victim selected is either excluded from the group, or punished through psychological or physical violence – even death. The reasons for selecting one victim rather than another will often have less to do with any genuine responsibility for the ills afflicting the group than with the fact that the victim in some way stands out from the rest. Once the act of exclusion has been performed, the social group enjoys respite from its internal stress until new conflicts arise and a new victim must be sought. For Girard, this mechanism lies at the origin of many social and religious structures. It is why the rituals of sacrifice emerge in human society. Because the phenomenon of 'scapegoating' is a universal one, it offers theologians the beginnings of an explanation for why the sacrifice of Christ, as the divine victim of the mechanism, might have a universal significance.

171

That a mechanism like this operates more or less subtly in some form in all human social groupings would be hard to deny. However, whether it is the root of all human evil is questionable, and whether it is what all sacrifice is really about is also debatable. But it does offer us a way of understanding how God might act in human history to work through and transform a fundamentally evil social structure. Human sacrifice is replaced by animal sacrifice and animal sacrifice is replaced by the sacrifice of the will. The individual now takes his share of the responsibility for transforming the situation of the community and no longer tries to escape it by projecting his guilt onto another.

More importantly, though, we can see how God, through his Son, directly confronts the evil reality of collective violence that underlies much of human activity, concealed by the mask of righteousness. Raymund Schwager reads the Gospel narratives as a drama in five acts, demonstrating how, through the power of God and the generosity of Jesus the mechanism of violence concealed beneath the mask of justice is attacked and overthrown from within. First, Jesus proclaims the Kingdom of God, a new order in which a new community turns to God, abandons violence and resigns the right to judgment one over the other. Second, when the message of the Kingdom is rejected by the religious leadership, which refuses to acknowledge its collective sin, Jesus, as prophet, proclaims the judgment of God against them. Third, Jesus falls victim to the spurious judgment of that leadership. He is judged, condemned and killed by the mechanism that transfers collective blame for the ills of the community onto the one who has identified those ills. In the fourth of

Schwager's Acts, the resurrection of Jesus proclaims the definitive judgment of God in his favour, which is at the same time a judgment of forgiveness; and in the fifth and final act, a new community is gathered through the Holy Spirit in which the values of the Kingdom will be made real.

So the violence of the collective fails before the power of life; the judgment of the priests (he has blasphemed) is refuted by the risen one, who is the just one. If we view that collective violence as the sum of individual guilt, projected onto the chosen victim, then Christ really does die as a result of the sins of the world and has to do so as a human being if he, as God, is to transform humanity. God is thus bound to work within a mechanism which he has not directly willed as a consequence of things he *has* directly willed (free will among human beings).

This is a very powerful way of understanding sacrifice and salvation. But it is not without its problems. Some have already been mentioned. Firstly not all sin is collective sin and not all collective sin entails victimisation. Secondly, where there is individual failure, the collective very often needs to make a response and sometimes the most appropriate response, for the good of the collective, is exclusion. But is the victim then a victim in the sense we have discussed so far? Finally, and most dreadfully, Christians collectively have a terrible record over the centuries for racism, intolerance of difference and xenophobia, which suggest that if the Kingdom is indeed being made real in history, we must think of its development and growth as partial and non-linear.

If we are to understand the language of salvation (rescue), it is worth thinking more widely around the question: what do we need to be rescued from? Liberation theology draws our attention to the suffering, poor majority of humanity with whom Christ identifies in his preaching, suffering and death. Rescue here means liberation from the political and economic oppression of a powerful and selfish minority. Moments of such liberation in history are signs of the deeper liberation in the resurrection. Girard's theories, as we have seen, point to a rescue from the powerful mechanisms of collective violence. In both cases the perpetrators of violence themselves need to be rescued from the blindness that prevents them from seeing their own sin, just as the addict needs liberation from the substance that enslaves him. The sick need liberation from their illness. Those conscious of guilt and failure need liberation from the debts which they know they cannot repay and their own helplessness. All humanity needs rescue from the destruction of death.

But all these things belong to the limits that our existence in a particular body, culture, family, community and personal history places on our freedom. Our past choices limit the freedom of our future choices for good or for ill; culture and false consciousness limit our ability to imagine the pathways that make real the glory of God. Infirmity and oppression can crush us and prevent us living fully human lives. At some point, even in the happiest and most fulfilled life, a human being encounters his or her own limits, the limits determined by existence on the timeline of this world.

It is in personal encounter with those limits and, above all, in the moments when we realise our own deep inability to undo or make good all that we have done badly, that we can acknowledge our need of God and discover the deep rescue that Christ brings by bridging the incompleteness of our world of time and opening for us the freedom of eternity, the world of God-time, in which wrongs can be righted and reconciliation can be real. Such moments are moments of conversion, an encounter with a powerful reality in which our self-understanding and our aspirations are reforged. Such encounters are foundational to the reception of the Christian message, whether in the powerful experiences of Paul, Augustine and Luther, or the simple, liberating encounter at the side of a lake. Christ has walked through and touched the whole of human life and the rescue that he brings will touch different people at different moments in different ways: a blind beggar, a woman about to be stoned to death, a tax-collector, a campesino, a bandit, a bishop. In the moment of encounter we begin to learn from him the ultimate pathway to freedom, to hand our limited selves over and to find our true selves in God.

Anselm and Athanasius are right. The Word that shapes us and our universe, the one in whom we are called to live and move and work for the glory of God, had to become human to open for us that life of God-time, which completes us. Only the *Word's* humanity could be essentially bound to our humanity, so that, as she breaks through the mechanisms that imprison us, her life, death and resurrection can bring liberation for us all.

The Way

Christians who accept the salvation of Christ are challenged to live out the values of the Kingdom in time. For Catholic Christians, this is done in the context of a Church community whose structures and whose teachings have evolved in history. Yet this is not without its difficulties. In the next chapter we will complete this cycle of reflection with a discussion of the Way.

Chapter 12: The Christian Way

In the Roman Catholic Church those who are guardians of the mysteries are also guardians of morals. Those who cannot keep the rules of the community are excluded from full participation in the mysteries by the guardians. There is, as a result, a source of conflict when the official Church tries to operate in a culture which prizes individual liberty and rational choice. In the western tradition of the enlightenment, a rule must justify itself rationally before it can expect to be taken seriously by free rational beings. However, in the tradition of the Church, the fact that a rule issues from the competent authority is sufficient reason for it to be obeyed, irrespective of whether the arguments justifying the rule are found cogent by members of the community. The encyclical 'Veritatis Splendor' dispels any doubt on this matter.

As a result of such conflicts many people who in other respects might quite like to be Christians find themselves on the wrong side of the line, defined as sinners and only able to approach the Eucharist and share in the life of the community with a bad conscience or not at all. Those who have entrenched differences with the Christian community or its priestly authorities can often assume that they have the same entrenched differences with God. Yet if the image of God we have been using thus far is correct, it is never possible to be outside the boundary of God's love.

177

It is no accident that the major source of conflict is the area of sexual behaviour. If one were to ask the average person what Catholic teaching on ethics was, they would probably highlight no abortion, no condoms, no sex before marriage and no homosexual activity. In this regard, the Church has been true to the Jewish tradition from which it springs. Josephus, highlighting the distinctive facets of Jewish living in the first century AD picks out, among other things, large families, no abortion and no homosexual activity.

In the course of the centuries the rules on these matters have been justified by reference to natural law arguments: the purpose of sexual behaviour in nature is reproduction; the laws of nature reveal the will of God, therefore it is the will of God that sexual behaviour should only occur in order to achieve reproduction. Again, this strict interpretation of the (single) purpose of sexual activity is recorded by Josephus among the Essene sect, whose marital practice reflects this understanding, and remains in the Catholic tradition until the encyclical Casti Connubii, in which it was allowed that sexual activity might also enhance the love between man and wife. Unlike the Essenes, the majority of married Catholics had probably anticipated this modification of the teaching for the best part of two millennia.

And of course, sexual behaviour is one of the areas – and a deeply critical one – in which modern people expect to be allowed to exercise their discretion. If authority tells me that I cannot do something that I both want to do and can see no good reason not to, then so much the worse for authority. This is not a culture in which the sacrifice of the will comes easily - which is not to say, of course, that there is no consensus on sexual norms: some people would agree that adultery is a bad thing (although this would not necessarily stop them committing it); some people find homosexual behaviour unacceptable; there is universal condemnation of paedophilia. However, there is little firm moral support in western culture for the absolute position in the range of sexual matters taken by the Church. In a culture of tolerance, it is much harder to take a counter-cultural decision, especially when the reasons for doing so seem obscure.

But this impression of Catholic teaching is misleading. It is accurate as regards content, but to focus on this area grossly distorts the picture of what is at the heart of the Christian Way, and what the real, deep-seated problems of following that way are for modern people.

The Deeper issues surrounding the Christian Way: An ethic of perfection or of invitation?

If we are looking for the root of our problems with the Christian Way, we might start with how it is presented, both in the New Testament and by the Church, as the ethic of the redeemed. It is the way of life to be followed by those who have been baptised and accepted the teachings of the Lord and of his Church. In theory, as participants in the new covenant, enlightened by the Holy Spirit, the baptised should be able both to accept and to keep the laws of God,

179

which are now written on their hearts. They should not need brother to teach brother. Practically, however, there is a gap between our status as redeemed and our ability to walk the way of the new life. This is not a new discovery: Paul has to remind the Galatians, 'if we live in the Spirit, let us walk in the Spirit'. But there is a conflict between the logic of this ethic and our own experience of ethical failure. On the one hand, because the ethics of the redeemed is an ethics of perfection, it makes sense eventually to cast out of the community those who cannot conform to its expectations: those who cannot keep the rules clearly do not have the Spirit and clearly do not really belong. On the other, though, who, in the real world, keeps the rules to perfection?

Yet if we look more closely at the teaching of Jesus and at the range of his instructions, we gain a slightly different perspective. Much of what he says turns out to be about the cultivation of interior dispositions: to practise chastity of mind; to practise letting go of anger; to be ready with forgiveness; to refrain from judging one's fellows; not to be dependent on possessions. Of course the dispositions relate to particular patterns of behaviour, but these patterns are not clearly defined in advance; rather, they are still to be lived out according to the new dispositions within. There is no neat fit here with the older model of sin and virtue as violation of or obedience to a determinate set of rules. Perhaps the most important of the dispositions is the continuous acknowledgement of one's dependence on God for life and mercy. Beyond these, there are positive commands to renunciation, to embrace lack of possessions with Christ, to be able to surrender oneself for the sake of the Kingdom.

Such instructions were then, are now and probably always will be counter-cultural. But strangely, in their case, it does not make them unappealing; it just makes them difficult. Christ is asking for a transformation of the self and is asking his followers to take personal responsibility for their own transformation. It is the letting-go of self entailed in this transformation and realised in every aspect of daily life that is the real ethical 'wall' at the heart of the Christian Way – not a small subset of specific rules. This inspiring and challenging aspect of the Christian Way, which is at the heart of the matter, is not, unfortunately, the first thing one thinks of when one hears the words 'the moral teaching of the Church'.

Again, if we focus on that subset, we neglect the mystical aspect of the Way, which derives from the teaching that Jesus is the living Word of God. The transformation that is called for is a transformation to become like Christ, who not only teaches us but also embodies for us what it is to be truly human. The determinate commandments of the written Law are fulfilled and transcended by a person who demonstrates the way he proclaims in his own life and death.

The importance of this shift in perspective is twofold. On the one hand it transforms the pursuit of ethics into an engagement with another person and the acquisition of a new character, a new way of being human. Walking the Way is done in a dialogue of friendship with the one who is the source of life – an idea already familiar from the Old Testament prophets: we are invited to become what our companion is. On the other, the good life is not defined by a determinate set of rules for behaviour, but by a space whose contours are only partially revealed by such rules, in which the Christian imaginatively searches for the will of God. The written precepts are the book that we pick up to guide us around the same room that we have always lived in, while the person of Christ leads and inspires us to undertake a journey into the unknown. This ethic is an ethic of invitation, the invitation to Levi, Zacchaeus and the fishermen. Jesus breaks bread with them without waiting for them to become perfect.

In practice, the Church has learnt to acknowledge that the Christian Way must be lived as an ethic of invitation rather than an ethic of perfection. The precepts are stated clearly, but it is recognised that people fail, and the sacrament of reconciliation exists to offer a way back. Indeed, the experience of the centuries has shown that moral failure and forgiveness can be important moments of growth. The pathway of the prodigal son, which leads to a deep understanding of the forgiveness of the Father, is just as valid as that of the obedient elder son.

But if there is freedom on our journey, there is also a duty for the good Christian who finds himself or herself in conflict with a precept of Church authority to reflect, pray and meditate over the precept and to ask where (s)he is being led. We need to find a certain detachment from our own desires and from the assumptions of our friends and newspapers if we are to make genuine, free decisions. Equally there is a duty on the part of the Church authority to present the authentic teaching of the Church in a way which does not foreclose on the discernment of the individual, which recognises that individuals are still in relationship with God, irrespective of their position on a particular ruling, and which presents this particular issue as a part of the wider issue of the integrity of the Christian life.

The way the Church talks: The quality of the Church's ethical language

But there is another aspect to the way in which the Church deals with ethical issues. Often we appear to talk in terms of a right and wrong that are determined simply by obedience and disobedience. We give the impression that ethics is a simple, binary system. This is the complement to the ethic of the redeemed that the Church tends to preach in public: you must keep a finite set of precepts in order to remain in the community, and if you fail in any one of them then you must be excluded. Happily the Church is less swift than before to consign all those guilty of serious infringement to damnation, but the juridical structure of exclusion remains clear.

The binary ethic raises three different sets of problems. One is that it appears to remove the *quality* of the infringement from consideration. It is not wrong because it is this kind of action but because it is an act of disobedience. In practice, though, the quality of ethical failure (and success) is important and needs to be considered when working out the due response to that failure. A second problem is that it hits hardest where definitions are clearest, and yet there are many activities whose definition is more difficult but which arguably deserve to be hit far harder than those which provide easy targets. It is easier for the Church to denounce the man who cohabits with his

183

girlfriend than it is for it to denounce the former head of a totalitarian state. Finally, the binary ethic does not distinguish clearly between simple sinful acts and complex life situations in which sinful acts are repeated as a matter of course.

Let us take the first point first. When we look at the quality of ethical transgressions (this is wrong because it is murder) we look beyond the boundary defining the particular kind of wrong action (unlawful, intentional killing of a fellow human being) to the complementary vision of what is right, which implies an ideal picture of human relationships and of human character. We are led to contemplate the virtues we are called to share in imitation of Christ. We see what the wrong action negates and why it leads away from God.

Humanae Vitae: a case study in non-binary ethics

This treatment can be instructive if applied to *Humanae Vitae*, whose precept outlawing the use of artificial contraception is arguably the most discussed and least observed in the Roman Catholic repertoire. The words of Paul VIth refer to the use of artificial contraception as 'intrinsice inhonestum', though this is reported in a later encyclical of John Paul II as 'intrinsice malum'. Now the latter word 'bad' is a binary word, and perhaps reflects the fact that subsequent treatments of the matter have more to do with the defence of magisterial authority than with the actual issue of the use of contraceptives. But Paul's word 'inhonestum' is more interesting, or can at least be read as such. It can be translated as 'disgraceful' or 'shameful', but its complement is the

184

virtue word 'honestas', honour, integrity, nobility. This reading gives a much richer understanding of Paul's position. His picture suggests that resort to artificial contraception is an attempt to cheat God, in whose hands lies the gift of all life within the universe. There is a lack of integrity in the relationship with God implied in the action.

At once there is richer material for reflection and discernment for the individuals who have to decide whether or not to accept the teaching of Paul on this point; but more significantly this approach also raises questions about the most appropriate response to a transgression with this particular *quality*. In the binary system it is clear: exclusion from communion. But as soon as we consider quality we are bound also to consider what course will lead people forward in their relationship with God. The case of someone who has committed a murder will be very different from that of someone who uses artificial contraception. The term 'intrinsice malum', which applies to both, does not help us to see any distinction.

The Church and the difficult targets

In complex ethical matters, the list of precepts is necessarily incomplete, and the temptation to use the simple labels of binary ethics is much reduced. In this field the Church has learnt and has moved a long way in its ability to talk about ethics on the political and international scene. It has been much readier to be consistent in pointing out acts of injustice by powerful individuals and governments than in the days when it was dependent on their goodwill for survival.

The late John Paul II was particularly impressive in this regard. There has been a high quality of reflection on questions of structural and global injustice that has taken the Church beyond the confines of the traditional, personal ethics of antiquity and given it a voice that can make a difference to the way humans live together on this planet. Institutionally, the Church has been led forward and Christians are made aware of the new dimension to their calling that has been opened up. The Church has also learnt to acknowledge collective, institutional sin in a way that would have been unsayable a century earlier. So there are indeed moves towards consistency and even-handedness in the moral judgments of the Church.

Situations beyond the boundary

Perhaps the most difficult issue to resolve is that of people who are living in irregular situations: couples living together unmarried, divorced people who have remarried without annulment, homosexual partners. The binary system condemns them all on the basis of individual acts performed within the situations in which they find themselves. What binary thinking cannot do is acknowledge that there may be much good and much virtue within those situations. Loyalty, commitment, love, generosity can all be found there, just as they can be absent from situations that are deemed regular. Equally, ties of acquired duty, loyalty and mutual respect – in themselves laudable things – can be a genuine barrier to regularising situations in the eyes of the Church.

The rhetoric is, of course not the same as the practice, though this is not much comfort to those who are hurt by the rhetoric. Practically, as has been said, the local church will often offer pastoral solutions (these will vary from one parish priest to another) that occasionally belie the official pronouncements.

Nevertheless, it seems unfair that the Church as a whole cannot acknowledge that particular people are, despite their situation, genuinely attempting to live the Christian Way and model their lives, as far as they are able, on that of Christ. A juridically irregular situation can nevertheless allow individuals to grow towards the Christian ideal just as, occasionally, a juridically perfect situation can prevent individuals from flourishing.

The matter might be resolved by honest dialogue with all interested parties, a collective discernment about guidelines for practice, a re-evaluation and rereading of the inherited tradition as appropriate. Here it might be helpful to alter our understanding of marriage or appropriate celibacy, to consider them as a 'counsel of perfection', as used to be done with religious life. The same perspective might be used with the precepts of Humanae Vitae. This would provide a way of accepting the confusion of situations in which modern Christians actually find themselves, while valuing the sacrifice of those who are able to commit themselves to the married or celibate state, or to obeying Paul VIth's instruction.

All of us, in some way, are limited in our just and imaginative exercise of freedom by our own weakness and by evolved social and economic structures that are sinful. We may not be in situations that are

187

labelled adulterous, but as voters in a rich democracy we are, for instance, playing a passive role in supporting collective global extortion and human rights abuse. Yet the Christian community continues to offer us comfort and to assure us that Christ is prepared to sit and eat with us, inviting us to be transformed and continue on the Way.

Ethics and Rules for Christians

0.   What follows is sketch of an ethical theory to supplement what has gone before. It aims to provide a picture of how ethical living might best be understood by Christians. It does not answer any difficult questions. It assumes, relying on the language-game theory of Wittgenstein, that there are ethical statements which can be true or false. It acknowledges that ethical language can do other things as well. As a Christian theory, it assumes that the ultimate reality of ethics is to be found in the person of Christ. It is a neo-classical theory in which virtues are considered logically prior to rules.

1.   Ethical rules are means to an end. They are not what are primary in ethics. They serve the complementary functions of educating members of a society towards patterns of behaviour that are good and admirable and of protecting society and individuals from behaviours that are disruptive and destructive.

2.   What is primary in ethics is the quality of relationships expressed in particular actions and made real by those actions. The ethical character and motivation of the agent, the attitude of the agent to those affected by the actions, his/her ethical imagination are essentially bound to the actions and their effects. The primary ethical realities are virtues: courage, wisdom, generosity, kindness, self-control. Those who possess these qualities will move freely in a bounded ethical space. Where there are people living together in relationships defined by such qualities, there is the Kingdom of God.

3.   The specific actions performed by a generous person in one context will be different from those performed by a generous person in another context. However, these actions will have a family resemblance.

4.   The virtues are promoted by positive precepts, rules and sample behaviours (give your bread to the hungry) and negative (do not harden your hearts). Obedience to the commandments (thou shalt not kill) and other social rules is the limit of virtuous living.

5.   Some rules protect a society from disruptive and destructive behaviours. Animal and human groups have behaviour boundaries which protect the well-being of the group. Evolutionary ethics (systems emerging by trial and error, which practically allow a society to survive and function) and rational ethics (systems worked out beforehand by which a society might survive and flourish) converge.

189

However, there is more than one way of achieving a balance of advantages in any given group. As a result, structures and behaviours which are 'successful' for one group may be abhorrent to members of another group that has evolved a different set of 'successful' structures. Different societies have different behaviour boundaries. This is the problem of cultural relativism.

6.   Christianity, like many faiths and philosophies, supposes that there is a better way of being human, which implies that the behaviour boundaries of any given group are open to critique and transformation. This is true both for modern liberal societies and for traditional Christian or other religious societies. Rule boundaries can, and sometimes should, evolve.

7.   For Christians, the ultimate ethical reality is Christ, who, through his dual identity as human being and incarnate Word, both shapes and fills the ethical space in which we are invited to move. The space is not occupied by discrete, static objects but by subjects freely acting in relationship.

8.   To be obedient to the will of God is to heed his call to us to move creatively through ethical space, realising the virtues in the particular situations in which we find ourselves. Sometimes the highest act of virtue will be obedience to a rule. Sometimes the greatest failure in virtue will be obedience to a rule.

9.   Rules are maxims that incompletely bound the ethical spaces labelled by the virtues (justice and generosity, for example). Some rules are simple, some are complex. Some appear absolute, holding in every possible situation they define, while some are 'for the most part'. In general the simpler (less specific) a rule is, the less easy it is for it to be absolute. However, the simpler it is, the more powerful it is as a sign, a building block in ethical education for the training of affective and ethical sensibilities. We learn to love what is good and to hate what is bad, and rules are a part of that learning. We also learn to fear transgression. Simple rules often *feel* absolute. This gives them their power in protecting society.

10.   The end of ethical education is not to create people whose actions conform to rules, but people who freely choose to live creatively in ethical space. Their right judgment will be exercised in the spirit of the law-giver, even when the case has not yet been defined. This is what Aristotle calls 'epeikeia' and Thomas Aquinas, 'prudence'. This is why it is correct to talk of situation ethics and why discernment (the prayerful search for the will of God) is an essential part of Christian prayer.

11.   The ultimate ethical norm (rule) is 'the will of God for me (for us) now'.

12.   The community has a duty to formulate new rules for new situations. This is an act of collective epeikeia. The ability of the

community to integrate a new rule into their lives will be an important means of evaluating its worth. Examples of areas in Catholicism where new rules for new situations have been explored are in the areas of birth control, genetic experimentation and euthanasia.

13.　　Simple rules prescribing or outlawing simple act-types will not be adequate to every situation. The full evaluation of a case considers context, goals of agent, motivation and conflicting duties and responsibilities. That is why practical legal systems evolve case-law and casuistry. It can sometimes be more helpful to look on rules like the Ten Commandments as a summary of a body of case law under specific headings rather than as principles from which the rights and wrongs of specific cases are deduced.

14.　　The simple rule is a line in the sand. Properly acting, virtuous agents may find themselves (apparently) on the wrong side of that line at times (Jean Valjean).

15.　　The simple rules have a powerful symbolic value. It is easier for us to be trained in fear, delight, horror with regard to the simple. These signs then help us correctly navigate the bewildering waters of life.

16.　　Those who keep rules faithfully are admirable. This is the virtue of integrity.

17.   Perhaps a rule tells us this, minimally: 'if you cross this line, the probability that you are acting in accord with the will of God is low.'

18.   The probability will be different for different rules. Tried and accepted rules that come out of antiquity will have a different status from rules formulated within living memory, whose reception in the community is still being explored.

19.   There are, of course limits, on human freedom, which make it difficult to accept new rules and to envision the need for new rules. We grow up within a functioning ethical system and, by and large, learn to share the aspirations of our community and to accept the boundaries (not without a struggle) inherited.   When these boundaries are themselves unethical - in groups that tolerate slavery, racism or unjust economic structures - it requires a prophet to challenge the modus.

20.   Guidelines for evaluating the 'depth' of a rule that I find difficult: To what extent does it protect the life and well-being of my neighbour?   To what extent does it protect the integrity of the relationship between me and my neighbour, me and my God, me and myself?

21.   Human freedom is shaped by an ethical vision that is dependent on emergent structures – biological, social, political and economic.   These structures are not, however, themselves always ethically shaped.   In this sense, a community's vision is limited by

'original sin'. Its choices, decisions, ways of desiring, goals and aspirations are not entirely free to harmonise with the will of God. Its response to prophetic challenges may be less than perfect. King Ahab finds it hard to listen to Elijah. Paul's lists of behaviours unbecoming were intended for communities that did not always find those boundaries easy to appropriate.

22.   The great ethical training systems of the Stoics, of Buddha, of Epicurus, of Jesus of Nazareth force us to look not just at types of action (act-types), but at what is within us, what leads us to such actions. Such self-knowledge is the first step towards freedom.   In our metaphor, it is in the genuinely free exploration of ethical space that true happiness and fulfilment are to be found.

23.   For Christians the ethical space is filled by Jesus, died and risen, the embodiment of the Word. He is the first instance of the Way, and in our relation of friendship with him, we are transformed and ourselves become instances of the Way.

24.   The rules that our tradition gives us, even those we do not understand, are worthy of respect. They are signs that there are things more important than my immediate hopes, longings and aspirations. Where I have difficulty with a rule, I must meditate and pray and try to understand the structures that lead me to resist the rule. I must also try and understand the structures that lead the authority to affirm the rule.

My deepest desire must be to seek the will of God by the example of Christ. To move in ethical space.

25.   Where such a dialogue, sincerely conducted, sincerely fails, it must be remembered that ultimate decisions about salvation belong to God. Our rules, however long-established, are lines in the sand of events.

26.   The possibility of ultimate failure must remain real. It is possible to cut ourselves off from God-time by allowing ourselves to remain in the prison of inherited structures, by failing to pursue what is good, by becoming absorbed in ourselves. We can close ourselves off from the realm of the Word.

27.   Hell is the everlasting awareness of the loss of eternity. Its fire is the knowledge of the failures that cannot be undone. Its ice is the absence of faith, hope and love in an everlasting time alienated from God.

28.   The model of salvation presented here does not require an explicit acknowledgement of the name of Jesus. It does require a desire and commitment to live a life which is related to the Way.

29.   The community of Christ on earth attempts to incarnate the Way. When it does so, it is admirable. It reveals the transforming power of God's Word and shows that this is desirable.

30.　　When the community of Christ fails to be admirable, is unjust, hypocritical, authoritarian and unfeeling, it fails to proclaim the truth and undermines its own authority to formulate new and challenging rules.

Chapter 13   Reading the tradition (2)

The end of history

The 'script' handed to the first generation of Christians suggested that Jesus would return soon to complete the work of the new creation, and to reign forever. Yet, already within that generation it became apparent that things were not going to be so simple, and Christians had to try to make sense of a history that continued.

The difficulty in writing such a continuing history was (and is) that its climax – the resurrection of Jesus – is (in our time) past. Christian historians have tried to capture something of a continuing salvation narrative through accounts of the spread of the Gospel. So Luke begins the Acts of the Apostles with Peter preaching in Jerusalem and ends with Paul preaching in Rome. Eusebius, who writes his history of the Church in the era of Constantine, charts the progress of Christianity from its beginnings in the Middle East, through the twin challenges of heresy and persecution, to its glorious and peaceful recognition as the true religion that alone preserves the Roman Empire. In his final chapters, Eusebius finds recent Christian history foreshadowed in the Old Testament narratives of failure, punishment and restoration that lead to the return from exile in Babylon and the rebuilding of the Temple (1 and 2 Kings, Ezra, Nehemiah). Indeed the bulk of the last chapter includes his own oration to Paulinus, Bishop of Tyre, 'on the building of the Churches', which celebrates the newly granted freedoms of the Christians and makes explicit the prophetic link with the rebuilding of Solomon's Temple by the Jews after the exile in Babylon.

And yet Christianity, once established as the religion of the West, struggles to find more than partial narratives that show signs of salvation in a long and complex history. In the end it is in the lives of individuals (the Saints) that Christians look most often to see salvation history at work.

Perhaps for this reason, the larger history of the Roman Catholic Church is read most often as a history of doctrine, or of doctrinal disputes and their resolution. According to this reading, the progress of the Church is a process of ever-finer revelation of truth that has been proclaimed at all times and in all places by everyone. That truth has been contested by a succession of heretics throughout the ages, who have been successfully defeated by the power of the Spirit, so that the deposit of faith can be preserved for future generations.

This narrative is powerful, appealing and consoling, but it is also misleading. It ignores the diversity of understandings that have been held in good faith and without challenge by different Christians co-existing within the Church at any one time in its history. It also ignores the fact that Christians at any one point in history can, quite properly, reread the whole tradition thus far in response to the experience of their age, just as the disciples of Jesus reread the Old Testament and the tradition of the Jews. This is, of course, the exercise which the last few chapters have endeavoured to illustrate. Each new reading is capable of bringing about a transformation in the whole.

History, heretic and magisterium all have a role to play. Let us rehearse some of highlights of this process.

A history of transformations

When disputes about the divinity of Christ were causing civil disorder in the cities of the Eastern Roman Empire, the newly Christian Emperor Constantine called the bishops together at Nicea in 325 CE and asked them to resolve the issue. The council, convoked under the authority of the Emperor (interestingly not of the bishops, let alone of the Bishop of Rome), produced a document, which is the basis for the Creed recited each Sunday. Within four hundred years reverse typology had worked, the Emperor was officially the 'anointed of God', the 'new David'. The process we saw beginning with the letter of Clement and continuing through Eusebius reaches a new high point: the Old Testament provides a prophetic model, a type, for the Christian world order. The Christians become a people who have their Messiah and leader on earth. The structures of Christianity come more and more to echo religious and political structures from the Scriptures. The High Priest in the Temple in Rome becomes the leader and ultimate spiritual authority over the People of God. Rome can be read as the New Jerusalem on earth, its papal Temple a place of pilgrimage, where sacrifices are daily offered for the well-being of the Christian world. There is a tribe of priests – though chosen, not born – and the armies of the Christian monarchs are the armies of the Lord.

So after a thousand years of Christendom, the French Revolution was clearly a satanic attack on the natural social and political order, decreed by God. Accordingly, the revolutionary movements, attacking Church and Crown were bitterly resisted through the 19th and early 20th Centuries. And yet because of those ungodly movements, the magisterial Church was forced to learn, to listen differently to the voices and concerns of the poor and to recognise and respond to the reality of social and economic injustice. By being deprived of political power, it learnt once more to live without kings and without kingdoms – as Christianity was in the time before Constantine. Of course, the Churches have always had prophets of justice, but now they can read more freely the radical message of Jesus and the prophets. Set free from the chains of political establishment, the Roman Church has rediscovered its prophetic duty to speak out against unjust authority, tyranny and oppression. It has also been taught by a world intolerant of hypocrisy to recognise, acknowledge and atone for its own collective sins.

The cultic practices of Christianity have also evolved in time as it has moved into different cultural contexts. We are familiar with the seasonal Christianising of Yule and Easter. But similarly the honour paid to the Mother of the Lord in the early Christian tradition tames and Christianises the cult of the Mother Goddess in the Near East and across Europe. In this process, however, Christian theology and prayer are transformed. Mary becomes, like Jesus, a mediator; her honour is hardly distinguishable from worship, an honour which feminises the divine realm otherwise occupied by the masculine Trinity. Again like

200

Jesus, she is the focus of intense spiritual relationships. In the Catholic world she is often the figure who is reported to appear and speak in the name of God. The boundaries of traditional understandings of the divine are blurred when confronted with the human reality of this cult, a confusion which evokes differing theological responses. The Protestant revolution rejects the cult; the slower Catholic revolution tames it with careful theological phrases until it squeezes it within the boundaries of the mainstream teaching on salvation.

Then there are the theological revolutions. As the Roman Empire in the West collapses, Augustine challenges the extreme teaching of Pelagius the Briton on free will. Reaching deeply into the New Testament tradition, he affirms that the grace of God is necessary for human beings to do God's will. It is by his grace that we are saved and alone we can achieve nothing. Luther, rereading Augustine at the end of the Middle Ages, and rereading the scriptures in that light, begins a revolution that challenges the authority of the leaders and the very practices of the Roman Church. It is faith that saves – salvation cannot be earned by anything we do. For him, reading the Bible highlighted the stark difference between the Christianity of the New Testament and the Christianity of the sixteenth century.

Luther is judged a heretic, yet his writing evokes a careful response in the Council of Trent, which moderates the 'merit' spirituality of common pastoral practice and produces a new and nuanced definition of the relation between God's grace and human freedom. But the debate is not ended by a definition. Luther's thought and challenge continued to echo in Catholic reflection. The liturgical

201

and ecclesial reforms of the Second Vatican council are, in part, the last, peaceful, stage of dialogue that began bitterly in the 16th Century.

In the early 20th Century, faced with the radical challenge to traditional Christianity posed by Darwinian science and evolutionary historical theories, Teilhard de Chardin tried to reconcile faith, evolution and palaeontology. He was exiled for his pains and banned from publishing. But his works are now accepted by the Church as valuable insights of their era. Evolutionary theory once denounced by magisterial authority is now (with reservations) affirmed by its successor.

Karl Rahner engaged with the secular philosophy of Martin Heidegger and developed, out of his understanding of spirituality in the traditions of Ignatius and the German mystics, a theory of the essential relationship between human beings and God. In the 1950s his writings were considered dangerous and he was silenced (along with other leading Catholic theologians). But subsequently, his insights enabled the fathers of the Second Vatican Council to acknowledge and articulate a 'new' truth: that salvation can be found outside the Church.

In this movement it can be seen how necessary alternative readings of the tradition are to the life of the Church. Without diversity there can be no growth, no development. The heretic proposes, the magisterium responds. Through (an at times painful) conflict, tradition evolves. New, and sometimes more helpful, lines are drawn in the sand.

For this reason it is misguided to attack magisterial authority. It is always legitimate to hope that the structures of that authority will continue to learn from the culture of transparency and accountability valued by those brought up under democratic regimes. It is at least as legitimate to work towards assisting that learning process. Nevertheless, the magisterium is necessary. It is easy for an individual or a school to propose a new insight, much more difficult to test that insight for authenticity against the tradition which the people of God have experienced as true and as enriching.

On the other hand, salvation history continues. Church structures have not always been just this way and need not continue to be just this way. The official reading of history at any one time is itself conditioned by that history, and is therefore incomplete. However much an authority may want to declare one reading authentic forever, it cannot ensure that all future generations will accept that reading. For it too, its words, decrees, councils and encyclicals, become a part of history that will be read and reread as each new generation endeavours to appropriate, renew and live out the gift from the past.

What are our core beliefs? How should we understand God? What is central to the Christian way? How should we organise the life of the Christian community? Can patterns of ministry change? How should we worship? Who is in a relationship with God and who is excluded from such a relationship? The alternative readings of the tradition which co-exist with official readings at any one time are vital and valid. The reality of Catholicism, its beliefs and its practices has always been pluriform. The Spirit moves in every limb of the body and is present in each pole of an evolving debate - although this can be forgotten by both sides. For God is greater, lying both within and beyond the boundaries of existing formulations, just as she speaks and saves both within and beyond the boundaries of the Roman Catholic Church.

The Kingdom of God

Finally it is important to see that Salvation History itself is not linear in its development. We can conveniently think of the evolution of Church structures and teachings in time as moving continuously in one direction. Yet the reality, as we have seen, is more complex. As people of this faith, all that we do is done now in a real relationship to the one who was a part of our history two thousand years ago, and our task in any generation is not to protect existing structures or defend a dogmatic system as such, but to become living signs of the Kingdom of God. This is the glorious and free new creation, that is hidden in the Word, the imagination of God and that continually breaks into our reality. The task unites us to all men and women who have responded to the call of God, irrespective of place, era or religious tradition.

Yet this activity is shaped by – though not determined by – the structures (political, social and cultural) of any one era. So there have indeed been moments throughout our linear history when aspects of the Kingdom have been revealed through individual Christians or through the Church as a whole. Equally there have been moments where decisions and actions in the name of the Church have made the Kingdom invisible to all but the keenest eyes of faith. This suggests that we need continually to reread our texts and to know our history, if

204

we are to avoid becoming trapped in a false understanding of time, a false understanding of tradition or a false understanding of truth. Above all we need to return, again and again, to that text which tells us, more than any other, who we are and how we are saved, the text which teaches and challenges us to follow the Word of God and to reveal the Kingdom in our here and now.

So finally, we turn to the New Testament, and ask how we can read this crucial text with modern minds and with integrity.

Chapter 14   Resurrection of the Word

All the words that have been written so far are inspired by one whose reality escapes us. For words and concepts are both a window on reality and the veil that we can never pierce, which prevents us from grasping things as they truly are. When they are woven together to describe people and events, and show their connections in a narrative, our tapestry is an interpretation of history that both reveals and conceals the story and the people at its origin. The textual strands that present us with Jesus Christ include the writings of the New Testament, two thousand years of theology, mystical experience, critical history and sacred art. Where, then, in all of this is the real Jesus? For we still want a sure correspondence between narrative and reality if we are to commit our lives and our hopes to this person and his way.

The Christian churches chose, a hundred years after the time of Jesus, those writings which they judged to be the most reliable and authentic expression of their faith. These included versions of the Jewish writings of the Law, the Prophets, History writings, Wisdom writings. They provide the narratives of salvation history, presenting texts through which the Jesus narrative is interpreted as the culmination of that history. But above all, the Christians selected from a larger field of writings the collection of Gospels and letters which we know as the New Testament. And this is the text to which Christians have turned and turned again for renewal and transformation, trusting in its authenticity and integrity as the Word of God.

It is then alarming when our confidence in this text is undermined by the criticisms of sceptical historians. Miracles are discounted. The true Jesus has been identified. The bones of the son of Joseph and Mary have been found. Not all the letters of Paul are written by Paul. The Gospel narratives include formulaic, genre writing. Luke and Matthew copy parts of Mark, but only selectively. John's Gospel is very different from the others. There are even other Gospels around with very different accounts of Jesus's life and teaching... So central is this text to the Christian self-understanding that any doubt sown in our minds about its reliability (whether through serious or sensational scholarship) weakens our faith.

History, science and security

Oddly it is the search for security in the text that has led to this uncertainty. We wanted to find the text of which we could say, 'of this we can be sure'. These events at least really happened, these words at least are words as he might have spoken them. We wanted to use reason, to test the reliability of evidence, to cross-check with alternative sources, to construct arguments based on rational probability. It is, then, no surprise that we could be confident, as historians, that Jesus was executed at the time of Pontius Pilate, but should discount stories about miracles, as formulaic, genre writing, based on exaggerated reports of a culture eager to believe wonders. The arguments of David Hume run very deep. Miracles can never be the more probable explanation for reports of miracles.

More recently, the success of science has provided a gold-standard for good theory, to which some historians have aspired. An example of the application of scientific method is provided by the American 'Jesus Seminar'. This school proposes a theory to account for the New Testament writings which meets the falsifiability criterion of Karl Popper: a valid theory must make clear what evidence would falsify it. The theory should be consistent internally and with the evidence so far available. The theory should be the simplest explanation of the available data. All the investigator then needs to do is to amass as much evidence as possible from archaeology and other ancient sources to see whether the theory continues to be supported or needs to be modified. If the theory is good, it should be able to anticipate certain results successfully.

So the working theory proposed by the Seminar is that Jesus was a wandering Jewish philosopher in the tradition of the Greek Cynics. These were philosophers who characteristically practised a critique of the prevailing culture. Their founding father was Diogenes of Athens, who famously lived in a barrel and told Alexander the Great to get out of his light. The Seminar finds evidence from contemporary Jewish/Near Eastern culture to support this model of Jesus' activity. Accordingly his radical and counter-cultural sayings can be relied on to be broadly authentic –further tools are needed for authenticating sayings in detail – while accounts of events such as miracles and resurrection should be regarded as improbable and non-scientific.

This way of doing history has a long tradition. Historians, ancient and modern (Thucydides, Tacitus and Gibbon) have, on

208

principle, excluded the miraculous from the explanation of historical events. The elaboration of a 'scientific method' is a late manifestation of a well-established genre. Yet the method cannot after all fulfil its implied claim, to prove that the remarkable or the miraculous has not occurred. This is because that conclusion is already contained in the assumptions of the method. The non-natural explanation will always be less probable than the familiar and the natural. No scientific history could ever show that Jesus was the Son of God, because science deals precisely with those explanations that do not refer to the intentional actions of supernatural beings

In fact, however, because all forms of history consider human intentions and plans, any historians who might claim to be doing hard science are deluding themselves. As was argued earlier, human affairs are chaotic and events arising from human choices are sensitively dependent on initial conditions. Equally, our typical *explanations* for human affairs, so far removed from the quasi-deterministic laws of physics, are also sensitively dependent: dependent on the evidence available.

From ten pieces of evidence I can construct a plausible narrative linking them together and providing the most probable explanation of that evidence. An eleventh piece of evidence can then suggest compellingly that I am *radically* wrong (think of Piltdown man). We make our judgments about probability on the basis of our experience, our culture and our expectations. We can form judgments which are both reasonable in the light of those probabilities and false. Probability cannot guarantee truth.

In fact, assent to or acceptance of any interpretation of history already involves an act of faith in the traditional assumptions which support that interpretation. A history that places its faith in the assumptions of enlightenment reason already supposes that reality can be fully and adequately described without stepping beyond the physical and the human. Such a history may contain lessons and examples, but beyond that, it holds no power over us. It may be a way of doing history which is the safest available, the one least likely to lead into dangerous illusions, but it cannot *prove* that its narratives capture all reality. That is the assumption of its secular, rational faith.

Salvation History

The Jesus narratives of the New Testament and the salvation history of the Old Testament are a radically different sort of history. This history is founded on personal encounters between human beings and God which transform the events of history into signs of her action. The narratives no longer consist of dead facts from which lessons may or may not be drawn: they bridge past and present; they are part of the medium by which members of the believing community encounter God in their own Now. The sacred history is a window through which we refract our present circumstances and see God active here as there, now as then.

The test of the ultimate truth of the Gospels is not the balance of probabilities – a test they are doomed to fail – but the vitality with which the texts continue to mediate an encounter with the elusive person who inspired their authors. Whatever 'facts' we could establish about the distant past would be ambiguous, constrained by rational probabilities. The continuing justification for accepting the interpretation of faith is that here, as throughout history, women and men continue to find life.

Truth, proof and authority in Galatians

Paul provides us with a powerful example of this sort of argument in the letter to the Galatians. The letter appears to be addressing a situation in which Paul's authority and interpretation of the Gospel have been challenged. A group of Christians has arrived promoting what must have been a common enough understanding for first generation Christians, namely that it was necessary to receive circumcision, to be a Jew, in order to receive the salvation from the Messiah. Paul had taught otherwise and the challenge to his authority provokes an aggressive response. Buttressing his argument with selectively chosen scriptural texts, he argues that circumcision and obedience to the Torah are not only unnecessary but even prejudicial to salvation. This hostile position will render Paul persona non grata in Jerusalem and Antioch – even after he wrestles to articulate a more nuanced position in the letter to the Romans.

But Paul's fundamental problem is that he was not one of the original witnesses of the life, death and resurrection of Jesus. He did not encounter Jesus, the man as the others did. A key argument, then, in justifying his claim to authority and *a fortiori* the authority of his teaching is that he had a vision – he encountered the risen Christ. This is what gives him the right to teach and what gives legitimacy to his message. He makes clear in the later letter to the Corinthians that he interprets this encounter as a meeting with the risen Christ, just like the encounters of all the other apostles and witnesses. The Gospel he heard made his own experience possible and was also confirmed by that experience. Again, when looking for signs of the authenticity of the message preached, he will point not just to sources, written or human, but to the manifestations of the Spirit present in the new communities as both product and proof of the truth that has been received.

History and the Christ of faith.

We can, then, rightly talk of a Christ of faith, the Christ experienced in the living communities as distinct from the Jesus that historical and literary methods can recover. Yet the tradition has believed that they are one and the same. For many modern theologians, as we have seen, the historical reality of Jesus is vital to a full understanding of our salvation.

So we need the tools of academic history. Even if it must remain agnostic about supernatural claims, this history can lead us to a richer understanding of the milieu in which Jesus walked and spoke, in which the message of Christianity was first preached and in which the first texts were written. The followers of the Word should not fear truth. As our understanding of that world increases, words and incidents we read take on new dimensions and depths, the veil lifts on the invisible past and we can approach more nearly the richness of the Son of God.

Genesis of a message

The historical foundation of Christianity and its message is the encounter between Jesus of Nazareth and those who became his followers and listened to his teaching. It is not a book – any more than the Law and the Prophets are the historical foundation of Judaism. For these followers, he offered a new interpretation of the Torah and as far as they could understand and see, he had the power to heal all kinds of sickness. He formed them into a community, using the phrase 'The Reign of God' to describe the beginning of a new era, a new way of living out God's will. He challenged some current ways of understanding the Law, including ways favoured by the Temple Judaism of the period. He was executed by the Roman authorities at the behest of the priestly leadership in Jerusalem. But after this a significant number of members of his community claimed to encounter him, individually and together. They regrouped and began to proclaim a message which included some of these elements: Jesus of Nazareth was the Messiah promised in the sacred writings; his whole fate was predicted in those writings. His death and resurrection freed people from sin and rescued them from the judgment of God. Those who received baptism in his name would be purified, would receive the Spirit of God and would be enabled to live the life of the new community of Jesus until this world came to its due end and all things were made new by God.

And who are his followers?

Clearly, Jesus' followers came from a variety of backgrounds: fishermen, tax-collectors, Pharisees, rich people, poor people. But there are important hints in the New Testament writings that his movement has, or comes to have, some association with elements of the 'protest' or alternative Judaism that we have referred to before. These are the forms of Judaism that contest and even reject the authority of the priestly aristocracy in Jerusalem, typified by the Essenes, the Qumran sect and, perhaps, by John the Baptist.

It may be significant, for instance, that Nathanael (in John 1), acknowledged by Jesus as 'truly an Israelite without guile', hails Jesus not as 'Messiah' but as 'King of Israel'. The ancient distinction between Israel and Judah (the land of the Judaeans, the Temple and Jerusalem) is upheld. In the Qumran texts the term 'true Israel' denotes those who are in opposition to the corrupt rulers of Jerusalem. A 'protest' connection may help make some sense of the ferocious antagonism between Jesus and the 'Judaeans' later in the Gospel (Chapters 8, 10), which has had such a devastating effect on the history of Christian-Jewish relations.

There are other indicators. The pattern of hospitality offered to the apostles as they are sent on their mission by Jesus shows some similarities to the welcome offered by some of the Essene sects to their fellows, as described by Josephus. The memorial action of the last supper replaces the sacrifices of the Temple as their efficacy comes to an end, and some have suggested that this meal Jesus shared with his disciples was an echo of the ritual meals of Qumran.

The theology used by the different New Testament authors shows a mixture of contemporary traditions. Belief in the resurrection of the body is Pharisaic, according to Josephus and Luke. The style of Jesus' discourse is often close to that found in Rabbinic texts. Though he often criticises the Pharisees, he talks their language. However, the sense of utter dependence on God for righteousness, which Paul expresses in Romans 7, is more in harmony with Qumran. The phrase 'Sons of light', which appears in the mouth of Jesus in Luke's Gospel is also typical of Qumran self-understanding.

From memories to notebooks

The first group of witnesses forms an alternative society partly within, but partly separate from, the existing structures of Judaism. But the message had to be passed to others, and for the first Christian missionaries beyond the immediate circle of Jesus' intimate friends, key information would be needed. They would need stories about the life of Jesus, as reported by witnesses, and selected texts from the Old Testament to throw light on, or be illuminated by, that story; but above all they would need teachings. The words of Jesus would provide vital, living instruction in how members of the new community were to organise themselves and live their lives in preparation for the dawn of the new era and the judgment of God. Besides this, they needed to show that Jesus was, indeed, the Messiah, and that the Messiah had, indeed, to die. The narratives of his trial and execution will have come to be critical in the apologetic task of explaining how the Messiah came to be rejected by the religious leaders.

In many cases early missionaries will have been able to work in part from memory, recalling words or events they had witnessed themselves, or things that had been passed on by word of mouth in easily memorable form. But some will have needed to carry notebooks with them, with versions of important 'sayings' material. Sometimes these might have been preserved as teaching in a context – a particular occasion when a lesson was drawn from a situation. Sometimes they might have appeared as isolated sayings gathered under common themes or key words for easy memorisation. Needless to say, this implies a wide variety of selections and versions during the first decades of Christian missionary activity. Traces of such variant originals can perhaps be found in the two different versions of the Sermon on the Mount (Luke 6 and Matthew 5 - 7) as well as in the letter of James. But there is (arguably) 'sayings' material scattered throughout the New Testament (though predominantly in the first three Gospels) which implies the existence of the kind of collections suggested.

In the opening chapters of Acts, Luke (its probable author) tries to capture something of the flavour of early missionary preaching. If this reflection is at all accurate, it shows that, once the connections between scripture and the life of Jesus have been made and a basic message of conversion and baptism has been preached, there is little need for complex theology. The preachers and their audience share sufficient background for further detailed reflection to be unnecessary, especially since they expect an imminent end of the age.

From texts to theology: the letters

But as the mission expands to Jewish communities outside Palestine and begins to address non-Jews as well, a bigger picture needs to be painted if the message is to be understood. Furthermore, some rethinking needs to be done as the promised judgment fails to materialise. It is, perhaps, no accident that the earliest writing in the New Testament is (probably) Paul's first letter to the Thessalonians, in which he writes to new Christians who are worried by the fact that some of their brethren have died before the return of the Messiah. Paul reassures them that the dead are not lost and that the end time will, indeed, take the form promised.

Later, the critical question arises of whether it is necessary to follow the Jewish Torah in order to be a Christian, in particular whether it is necessary for males to be circumcised. This stirs intense and combative theological reflection, as we have seen. When Paul writes to the Jewish Christian community in Rome, he modifies his violent stance of Galatians (where he rejects the Torah absolutely) for a more irenic stance, which affirms the value of the Law but emphasises the gracious action of God in making us righteous through faith in Christ's death and resurrection alone. Echoes of this debate appear in

217

Ephesians, which proclaims a new harmony, speaking of a 'new people' in a union of gentile and Jew. Acts offers us a sanitised account of this first major crisis to split the community of Jesus' followers.

In the letters to the Corinthians, we see Paul addressing the new problems encountered in a community with few roots in the Jewish world. Some members have cultural assumptions about social and sexual behaviour which are at odds with the Jewish-Christian norm. Others have a tendency to speculative, rational thought which risks undermining the saving message of Jesus Christ. Echoes of similar community struggles can be heard in the increasingly desperate pleas of the author of the letters of John.

In the letter of James we hear a voice speaking (arguably) in the language of the Jewish Christians. Ostensibly there is a critique of an oversimplified version of Paul's message that we are saved by faith in Christ alone. For James the slogan is: 'show me your faith and I will show you my works'. But more importantly, here, more than in the other letters, we find direct echoes of Jesus' teaching as it is reported in Luke and Matthew. It echoes the prophetic critique of the rich and powerful that rings through Hosea, Amos, Jeremiah and, in it, Jesus himself is read as the model of the just man, unjustly murdered by the rich and powerful.

The letter to the Hebrews, on the other hand presents us, as we have seen, with an extended theological argument. In the most elegant rhetorical development in the New Testament, it attempts to reconcile a Jewish audience to a new dispensation rooted in the law of sacrifice but superseding it. Christ is here read as the true High Priest who offers

218

himself as the true sacrifice in a heavenly realm of which the earthly Temple in Jerusalem was only ever an echo.

The imagery of victim, sacrifice and the heavenly sanctuary become central to the book of Revelation, in which Christians are encouraged to persevere through trials by contemplating present history against the backdrop of a cosmic struggle, ultimately controlled by God. They are invited to look to the judgment of their enemies and the glory of the new age. Early teaching about the end time is re-worked in the tradition of the book of Daniel, itself written at the time of the Jewish rebellion against the Greeks and clearly important to the protest of Qumran and to that of Jesus himself.

In their different ways, the authors of the letters use models from scripture and contemporary Jewish culture to interpret the story of Jesus. But it is not until the compiling of the Gospels that the different elements of Jesus' story are pieced together in a systematic way as a history in order to *show* rather than *explain* how that story resonates with the writings of the Jewish tradition. Each Gospel is, of course, limited by the texts and traditions available to the author. Each is shaped by the author's background and concerns as well as by the needs and understandings of those for whom he writes. Each is a history that both conceals and reveals its subject.

Interpreting the Gospels, and historical truth

One key feature of the Gospel writings is the juxtaposition of text from the Old Testament with words or actions of Jesus. We are invited to read these texts as texts 'about' him. Sometimes this is done explicitly: thus Matthew and John will often make the point by spelling out the quotation. Sometimes it is done implicitly. Luke, for instance, prefers to weave the references into his narrative and let the reader make the inference. In the infancy narratives and in the passion narratives the references are very dense.

In an obvious way this can disturb us. At what points are 'facts' being reshaped to fit, rather than being shown to fulfil prophecy? If we look at the report of Jesus' last words on the cross, we find in Matthew and Mark a cry of desolation, a quotation from Psalm 22. In Luke, however, we find a quotation from Psalm 31, filled with trust in God, while John has Jesus utter the triumphant, 'it is accomplished'. Are they all false, or (as devotional practice supposes) are they all true?

Of course, Jesus knew the Law, the Prophets and the Psalms intimately and was able to read his own destiny out of them. Accordingly there is no reason why he should not quote scriptures as he approached his end. The problem is how we could actually know what he said. The words are too convenient in their respective narratives and the narratives are too different from each other for us to trust them. Again, this unsettles us: if Jesus did not actually say these things, does that mean that the meaning they give to his death is a false one – or perhaps that his death means nothing at all?

It is, of course, always possible that his death means nothing at all and that Christianity is wrong, but whether or not he actually said those words makes no difference to that question. The authors of the Gospels are, in their different ways, attempting to convey what they believe to be the truth about his death. The words they put into the mouth of their dying messiah explain his meaning in the light of the scriptures. The raw data of his trial, punishment and execution say nothing until they are woven into a greater narrative: that narrative interpretation is what begins to show how these events are life-giving.

His very words

This is, though, part of a more general problem we experience with the words of Jesus: they are filtered in so many ways - in the passage from Aramaic to Greek; as they are shaped into memorable form; in their interpretation and elucidation for different audiences; in their expansion through exposition. Again and again we are inclined to ask: are these words then inauthentic? Are the Gospels unreliable? And the answer is – in a way, yes and in a way, no.

One of the features of the Semitic languages is that, like colloquial English, they can convey in compressed form ideas that are readily understood in context, but out of context require careful articulation to convey the sense. Such language is therefore highly ambiguous and, in articulating it, options are taken that exclude other potential meanings. In Luke's Gospel Jesus says 'Blessed are you poor', while in Matthew's Gospel he says, 'Blessed are the poor in Spirit'. Against the background of the Prophets and Psalms, the term 'poor' denotes *both* the oppressed *and* those who are humble before God. The letter of James, with the Gospel of Luke, takes a clear option and makes no bones about the fate awaiting the rich oppressors. Yet Matthew's

221

'poor in Spirit' is a valid articulation of the range of meanings of the word 'poor', which extends the scope beyond simple economic disadvantage.

Articulated, translated, elucidated, the words of Jesus can be authentic in two ways. First, they can convey the sense that Jesus most probably intended in context; second, they can express the sense appropriate to a situation which the original occurrence may not have envisaged. Here, the tradition has the use of a sort of epieikeia, or prudent judgment in the power of the Spirit. This is how Jesus might have used the words, or what he might have meant by them, in the context that now confronts his followers. The words live in the tradition and their meanings cannot be static, though it is always enriching to search for a most probable original meaning. Words, and the minds interpreting them, continue to be shaped by the Word itself.

Words beyond history

There is a further category of sayings attributed to Jesus, which are to be found above all in John's Gospel and in the book of Revelation. These may also be elucidations or expansions, perhaps of prophetic sayings from the collections. But there is a good case for saying that they are derived from contemporary prophetic experience of Jesus as the Word of God, the Lord who continues to speak through the communities or – in the case of John through the Gospel writer – in the here and now.

222

This disturbs us too, undermining our ordinary understanding of what we would mean by the 'Word of the Lord' – especially since such great weight is given to the 'very words' in the tradition (the critical modern teaching on divorce, for example, is founded on the 'very words' of Jesus). In the case of John's Gospel, when the words of Jesus seem to carry echoes of violent verbal clashes between Christians and Jews in the bitter process of separation in the years after the destruction of the Temple, we want to ask: is the Spirit really at work in this bitter hostility? Is this the authentic voice of the risen Lord?

The visionary presence in the book of Revelation is similarly disturbing. The vindictive agent of divine judgment seems a far cry from the man who preaches forgiveness and non-violence. True, the words of Jesus in the Gospels do promise the coming judgment of God: for some, there will be eternal life in the Kingdom, for others, eternal annihilation and exclusion. It is also true that when Jesus speaks of God's judgment, he does so in a language that echoes Jeremiah and Daniel. Revelations merely expands that language to include the history lived by the first generation of Christians in God's master plan and to affirm the rescue of his chosen by the blood of the lamb. Yet the lurid detail of the punishment of the enemy expresses a deep desire for vengeance that seems to owe more to the humanity of the writer than any truth communicated by the Spirit.

The living word is powerful and dangerous, expanding beyond a received text in the lived relationship between believer and Christ, opening to new insight, but open to diminishment through the limitations of the human hearer. It is an opportunity for human words to be reshaped in the hidden matrix of the divine Word, but always with the possibility that the new words spoken may be adulterated by false human understandings. What is true for Christianity is true for any religion in which revelation and prophecy play a part.

We need to be aware that such words, more than any other, need to be read in context. We need to reread them against our deeper understanding of a God of mercy who wishes to rescue and save all people. When Paul and the author of Acts write, they do so with hope that all people will eventually receive the saving word. In John 3, Jesus says 'God sent his son, not to condemn the world, but so that through him the world might be saved.' The words of hope seem more deeply authentic than the angry response to division, rejection, hostility and persecution found in John 8 and 10, or in Revelations 19.

Ultimately, though, it is the tradition that has produced and authenticated the words of the Gospels: they were written by members of Christian communities for members of Christian communities and accepted as reliable by the Christians of the 2nd Century. This tradition tells us: we, as believing Christians, can trust these words to be an authentic expression of our faith. But always, when they speak to us, they will speak in a new way into our new situation. These words are authentic - and they are alive.

The myth of the single author and community text

Each Gospel writer desires to present Jesus as the Messiah who preaches and heals, and who suffers, dies and rises to save his people from sin and death. Each Gospel in a different way, for a different audience, persuades the reader to recognise in Jesus the promised Christ, and to respond personally to his call. Yet not all the Gospels were written in one draft – and some might argue that none of them was. John's Gospel, in particular, seems to have undergone a number of transformations, perhaps with different hands involved. The single author is a helpful myth for giving authority to the product of a common enterprise.

That thought may dismay us, but it should not, if the argument about the relation between scripture and the living tradition is properly understood. These writings are the result of a gestation process from within the Christian communities which begins with the different preaching of the first missionaries and ends (though even there it is not ended) centuries later with the selection of our New Testament as the Word of God.

So it does not matter that many hands may have been involved, provided that at each stage of the process the communities can see mirrored in those words the essence of the faith they have inherited, and find in them a source of enrichment and renewal. We must remind ourselves too that what is true for other ancient documents is true for these as well: distance from events does not have to undermine reliability, a relationship to other sources does not have to undermine credibility and the absence of actual samples of pre-Gospel collections does not mean that they never existed when there are good textual reasons for thinking that they might have – the reason being that these texts are produced from within a continuously existing faith community. The narratives, the words, the events, the experience are present in the communities before they reach the page.

History revealing the Messiah

The Gospel narratives, as we have said, show the reader who Jesus is. They invite us, who are new to the faith, to see and know Jesus as the Christian community see and know him. We are invited to see in his life the fulfilment of prophecy and to hear in his words the message of a new way of life. Meanwhile, alongside the references to Old Testament scripture, the accounts of miracles ('powers' or 'signs') point us ever more clearly towards the truth, spoken by Peter on our behalf, that he is the long-awaited Messiah.

Thereafter, however, begins the challenge of showing how the Messiah firstly *must be* rejected and secondly *actually is* rejected. Mark, in particular, invites us to be one step ahead of the disciples as they fail again and again to appreciate and understand Jesus' words. Luke will suggest in his resurrection narratives that it is only after the resurrection itself that the disciples' minds are opened to understanding the scriptures.

We are led through the conflicts of the last week in Jerusalem. We experience the intimacy of the last memorial meal, before we witness the trial, suffering and execution. As the narrative weaves in echoes of prophetic text, we are invited to see, in this apparent horror and disaster, our salvation.

But can we read through this narrative to Jesus as he was? How aware was Jesus of the meaning of what he was doing?

Jesus' self-understanding:

The Gospel writers suggest clearly that Jesus had a sense of the script to which he was working and which his disciples failed to understand. When Jesus enters Jerusalem, his speech proclaiming the downfall of the Temple and the end of Jerusalem is fully in the tradition of the prophets (in e.g. Mark 13). Jeremiah, the prophet who witnessed the capture of Jerusalem and the destruction of the first Temple 600 years before, provides the clearest model. Indeed, the Gospels of Matthew, Mark and Luke make an explicit link between Jesus' cleansing of the Temple in his day and Jeremiah's speech in the original Temple (Jeremiah 7), where he denounces a liturgy as well as a leadership that rejoices in the Temple but fails to do justice.

Jesus is steeped in the scriptures, and we have seen how, in the culture of the time, prophetic texts could easily be read with contemporary reference. Jesus is in a position to see which way the course of prophetic protest will lead. He is also in a position to see Jerusalem faced with a threat not dissimilar to that posed by the invading Babylonians of the 6th Century BCE. It is not implausible, then, to claim that Jesus actually did read his own destiny in the scriptures and that his reading led him to speak and act as he did.

227

Explaining his death

The New Testament authors give a range of explanations for what Jesus' death accomplished. He died 'on our behalf' says Paul. Luke quotes from the key text, Isaiah 53, 'like a lamb he was led to slaughter'. He is the one who takes the sins of the people upon himself. John the Baptist (John 1) recognises Jesus as the 'Lamb of God'. The words of Jesus preserved in the blessing of the cup speak of the blood which seals the covenant, rooting his action in the foundation of the community of God in Exodus. In the ancient context, these different images help the reader to understand the meaning of this death.

But the Gospel writers in particular also give us an insight into the *mechanism* which brought about Jesus' death; how it was that he came to be rejected and killed. Jesus, like many of his contemporaries, interprets the Law of Moses. His style is in some respects very similar to that of other rabbis. However, his specific reading of the Law involves a movement away from a literal obedience to every commandment. Some commandments he radicalises: not only should you not kill, but you should not have within you the anger that leads to killing; not only should you not commit adultery, but you should not even look upon a woman lustfully. Others, however, he interprets generously. But in many encounters it is his interpretation of the Sabbath Law – one of the 10 most sacred commandments – which is presented as arousing hostility and suspicion of his credentials from his peers.

Another recurrent theme is his association with recognised 'sinners', and contact with people or things that were 'impure' – foreigners, a leper, a woman with a blood flow, a corpse. By such actions he seems to put himself outside the conventions about religious purity, at a time when purity was a matter of deep concern to many holy people. Further, and most significantly, he seems to have claimed the authority to forgive sins. Now his reading of the law is radical, challenging many of the standard readings of the contemporary Judaism, but if the claim to forgive sins is authentic – and it is (significantly) one that his followers claimed for themselves after him – then he is going far beyond the remit of a liberal rabbi. But still, so far, though we have seen how his words and actions might be offensive to local religious groups in Galilee, we have not yet seen why he might be of concern to the priestly elite in Jerusalem or to the Roman governor.

However, we have alluded to another strand of his discourse, in which he upholds the rights of the poor against the rich. This is clearly seen in Luke's version of the Beatitudes and Luke's parables about the rich. Echoes of this language also find their way into the Letter of James. Here, it seems, we have someone who is protesting against the established social order. This is compounded by direct criticism of the religious leadership implied in the cleansing of the Temple and the prophecy of that Temple's destruction. Jesus is challenging the contemporary interpretation of the priestly Law which binds the Law of Moses and the Temple cult to the cosmic order. He speaks with the voice of a prophet and looks to a salvation beyond the existing cultic order.

Through such words and actions, Jesus makes present the word of God, so that those existing religious and social structures may be challenged and transformed. That is why John explicitly speaks of Jesus as the Word of God, made flesh. That is why the author of Hebrews contrasts the message of the prophets with the presence of the Son. This living Word, who eats with sinners and touches lepers, demands inner purity of the heart and calls for renewal in a cult that has been corrupted and a leadership that fails to reveal God's Kingdom. For those leaders he is a threat and the threat must be destroyed. In John's Gospel (which uses the Greek form of the dialogue more than any of the others) as he stands before Pilate, Jesus is the martyr – the witness – for the truth.

The Jesus of the New Testament

So we have seen Jesus presented, *read,* as the Servant who bears the sins of the many, in whose death the world finds new life. He is the prophet, who fiercely denounces the religious and social elite and is punished for his pains. He is the righteous one, whose going seemed like a disaster, but who is now with God. He is the Son of David, the true Messiah and King of God's people, who will rescue his people and be exalted and rule all nations. He is the holy one of God, overthrowing the power of the enemy, the demons, sickness and death. He is the Son of God, sharing his likeness yet taking the form of a slave. He is the Word of God, the one through whom the universe was made, and in whom the universe finds its ultimate meaning.

Writing the Gospels, proclaiming the Kingdom, celebrating the Eucharist: None of these makes sense without the resurrection. That the Word of God fought with the powers of this world and overcame them can only be upheld if the resurrection is true. Paul was right: if the resurrection did not happen then Christians are the most unfortunate of people, who have lived a lie for the last two thousand years. And yet just here the uncertainty in the texts is at its height. The reports are confused, contradictory, blurring vision and solid reality. Mary is told not to cling, but Thomas is told to touch and believe. In Luke and John, Jesus eats with his disciples, while the earliest version of the Gospel of Mark ends with the discovery of an empty tomb. Where do resurrection encounters end and the visions of faithful Christians begin?

The nature of the event itself is a part of the problem, for it is not a miracle in the senses we have considered so far. It is not just an instance of a higher power either controlling unusually or actually altering the normal course of nature; it is, rather, a matter of revelation. The veil is momentarily lifted between this partial reality to which our understanding is adapted and a higher reality of which our world is just one aspect. In this regard, the resurrection has more in common with those strange revelatory miracles reported as walking on water or the transfiguration. Such revelatory experience is described in other religious cultures – in the Baghavad Gita, in Plato, in Islam – as well as in the tradition of Rabbinic Judaism. It is easy enough to talk of *visions*

231

– such experience is made of the stuff of dreams and hallucinations and does not commit us to a physical interaction with a higher world – but together, as has been argued, the traditional doctrines of the resurrection body, of the new creation and of the resurrection of Christ invite us to suppose a reality beyond the physical, and a reality to which we are already intimately bound.

Now if we were to experience a multi-dimensional timeless being in our own time and history, how would we report something which our senses are not adapted to comprehend? It would not be surprising if our reports were both confused and confusing. The strong Christian claim is that, in the resurrection appearances, certain favoured witnesses encountered just such a higher-order reality with an effect that changed their understanding of everything that had gone before. It is more probable, according to secular reason, whose parameters are the everyday, that they were lying or hallucinating or misunderstood. That statement cannot, however, exclude the possibility that they both told the truth as it appeared to them and were reliable witnesses of a unique phenomenon.

But the truth of the resurrection event cannot be judged alone by the conflicting and ambiguous encounters reported in the Gospels. Once again, the reports are validated by the experience of a living presence within the new community. Koinonia (a sharing of life) and the living friendship of which that is a sign are the things that confirm the truth of the Gospels. The power of the Spirit and the presence of the Son, the Word of God, must be encountered now. The Gospels are the narratives of a foundational encounter and their words mediate the transformation they describe to those who come after. The New Testament finds and stirs resonance in the lives of those who read it in a fluid structure of prayer, meditation, action and the common life of the community. It is reshaped in art, architecture, poetry, preaching and in people. In this sense, the New Testament continues to be written.

And we are invited to contemplate this Word as it embraces and shapes the universe it bears, present in the wretched and needy of the earth. We are invited to look and work and pray and rejoice and suffer the painful transformation of our selves and our communities in a history that unfolds in a dialogue with God, Father and Mother. We are called to open ourselves to the power of the Spirit so that we can read and speak and do the truth in our times. We are challenged to risk encountering for ourselves the risen one, Jesus, in light beyond light, in life beyond history, in the timeless revel of eternity.

Appendix 1

Some of the Dramatis Personae (in Chronological order)

Heraclitus: 5th Century BCE Greek philosopher who explained all physics with reference to fire and who used the term 'word' to define the divine tool with which the universe is steered.

Democritus: 5th Century BCE Greek philosopher who explained all physics with reference to atoms of different shapes and sizes moving in the void.

Plato: 5th/4th Century BCE Greek philosopher who discussed soul, reality, thought, goodness, politics and the afterlife. His philosophical language is very influential and was used by Jews and Christians in later centuries.

Aristotle: 4th Century BCE Greek philosopher who discussed everything from anthropology to zoology via ethics, logic and physics. His philosophical language is very influential in later centuries.

Stoics: 4th Century BCE onward. A school of philosophy that was influential throughout antiquity. While discussing physics and logic, their primary focus was, like Plato's, ethics and how to live the virtuous life.

Epicurus: 4th Century BCE Greek philosopher who derived his ethical theory from a variant of Democritus's atomic physics. Humankind should avoid pain and seek what is pleasant in a random and fragile universe. His is the forerunner of many modern, secular worldviews.

Qumran Sect: (2nd Century BCE – 1st Century CE) Radically religious Jewish group, probably based at Qumran near the Dead Sea, whose way of life is preserved in the 'Dead Sea Scrolls'. Their raison-d'être is a protest at the corrupted Temple in Jerusalem. They look forward to the revolutionary judgment of God.

Essenes: (2nd Century BCE – 1st Century CE) Jewish protest group described by Josephus, the historian, dating from the time of the revolt against Antiochus. One form of the Essene way seems very similar to the way of life described by the Qumran scrolls.

Pharisees: (2nd Century BCE – 1st Century CE) A group of working scholars who endeavoured to interpret the Law of Moses in the context of everyday life. Very influential after the Hasmoneans (the Maccabees) came to power.

Sadducees: (2nd Century BCE – 1st Century CE) A group based in Jerusalem that seems to have been associated with preserving the priestly cult on the basis of the Law of Moses. Famously, they did not believe in the afterlife.

Aristobulus: 2nd Century BCE Jewish philosopher in the Aristotelian tradition. Among other things, he attempted to reconcile the miracles of the Jewish Law with his Aristotelian understanding of physics.

Philo: 1st Century CE Jewish philosopher in the Platonic tradition. Among other things, he used the method of allegory to read into Jewish texts philosophical truths in the style of Plato and developed a theology of the Word.

Flavius Josephus: 1st Century CE Jewish historian. Josephus took part in the first stages of the rebellion against Rome at the end of the 60s, but surrendered to Vespasian. He wrote a history of that conflict and also gave a more detailed account of the history of the Jewish people for a non-Jewish audience. His writings provide the most extensive (though not always the most reliable) source for the different forms of Judaism lived out in the second Temple period (approximately 520 BCE – 70 CE).

The Rabbis: After the capture of Jerusalem by the Romans in 70 CE, Jewish scholars (rabbis) met together to decide how to continue practising their faith without a Temple. Their base must have included a large number of Pharisees, but the rabbinic writings show great diversity of interpretation. This movement marks the foundation of modern Judaism, and its tense relationship with Christianity, at first uneasy and eventually hostile, is mirrored in some writings of the New Testament.

Irenaeus of Lyons: 2nd Century CE Bishop who wrote against several heresies, in the process affirming the importance of the tradition as handed down through bishops from the Apostles and re-affirming the Old Testament as a document essential to Christian self-understanding.

Clement of Alexandria: 3rd Century CE Christian scholar who collected writings from the philosophers of antiquity to show that Christian truth was foreshadowed by all great thinkers.

Origen of Caesarea: 3rd Century CE Christian scholar who defended Christianity against the charge of irrationality in his tract 'Against Celsus' and used ideas from Plato and the Stoics to discuss and develop Christian theology.

Constantine the Great: (4th Century CE) The first Roman emperor to profess an interest in and actively support Christianity within the empire. He (and his successors) convoked the first ecumenical councils to resolve the doctrinal disputes between Christians that were posing problems for public order.

Athanasius of Alexandria: 4th Century Christian and Bishop. He was a key player at the Council of Nicea (325 CE), convoked by Constantine, in which the dispute over the divinity of Christ was resolved in the formula 'of one being with the Father'. He continued to defend this position through subsequent years in which the decision of the council was repudiated under Constantine's successors.

The Cappadocians (Gregory of Nazianzen, Gregory of Nyssa and Basil of Caesarea): A mutually supportive school of 4th Century theologians who developed the theology of the equal divinity of all three persons of the Trinity. In part because of their work, the creed of Nicea was reaffirmed at the Council of Constantinople (381) and was elaborated to include more substantial mention of the Spirit. This is the form of the creed we use on a Sunday.

Cyril of Alexandria and Nestorius of Antioch: Theological opponents in the 5th Century CE whose dispute concerned the relationship of the divine and the human natures in the person of Jesus. The dispute was temporarily resolved at the council of Ephesus (431) in favour of Cyril. But the arguments did not end until the council of Chalcedon (451), after the death of both parties, introduced the concept of the 'hypostatic union'.

Augustine of Hippo: 5th Century CE Christian scholar and Bishop who defended Christianity in the West as the Roman Empire came to its end, and laid many of the foundations of Western Christian thought (Catholic and Protestant), especially through his discussions of grace and free will.

Anselm of Canterbury: 11th Century CE monk who became Archbishop of Canterbury in 1093. He is most famous for a meditation in which he 'proves' the existence of God by ascending to a concept of God as 'that than which nothing greater can be conceived'. In 'Cur Deus Homo?'

(why did God become a human being?) he developed his own version of an argument of Athanasius, to show that humanity could only be saved by one who was both God and human.

Thomas Aquinas: 12th Century CE Dominican who engaged intellectually with the newly recovered writings of Aristotle, and used the philosophical language and style of Aristotle as a basis for expressing and justifying articles of Christian faith – most famously in the *Summa Theologiae*.

Martin Luther: 16th Century CE Augustinian friar whose rereading of Augustine and Paul led him, first, to call into question current trends in philosophical and theological thought and, eventually, to challenge the structures of Catholic Christianity of his era. In particular he rejected traditions and practices which were not founded on 'scripture alone'. This thesis provides the intellectual basis of the subsequent forms of Protestant Christianity.

Ignatius of Loyola: 16th Century CE soldier, mystic and priest who founded the religious order 'the Society of Jesus'. His spiritual exercises proved a powerful tool for renewal within the Catholic Church both before and after the Reformation had split the Western Church.

David Hume: 18th Century CE Scottish philosopher whose sceptical writings have had an enormous influence on British philosophy and (indirectly) on British intellectual culture. He was one of those who laid the foundations of modern empiricism (knowledge through sense-experience) and the positivism of modern science, as well as of agnosticism in matters of religion.

Immanuel Kant: 18th Century CE German Philosopher. His titanic work, 'The Critique of Pure Reason', seeks to justify the objectivity of scientific knowledge of the world, as codified by Newton in his 'Mathematical Principles of the Natural Order' over against the sceptical critique of David Hume. In the process he establishes that we can only know things as they appear to us (thus founding the family of philosophies known as 'phenomenology') and can have no knowledge of transcendent reality. In effect he provides a philosophical statement of the theological position of the 'via negativa' and affirms an essential division between religion (or 'metaphysics') and science – a position developed by the logical positivists of the twentieth century.

Appendix 2: Books that may be of interest (section by section)

Introduction

For a readable account of the British Enlightenment as a background to modern culture, see Roy Porter: Enlightenment: Britain and the creation of the modern world (Penguin, 2001)

Chapter 1: Future in the past and the development of truth.

Martin Hengel: Judaism and Hellenism (SCM, 1991)

John M.G. Barclay: Jews in the Mediterranean Diaspora from Alexander to Trajan (323 BCE – 117 CE) (Edinburgh, 1996)

E.P. Sanders: Judaism: Practice and Belief 63 BCE – 66 CE (SCM, 1992)

Chapter 2: A History of the Word

Chapter 3: A History of Being and other big words

For a general account of the Church history surrounding the developments discussed in these chapters see Henry Chadwick: The Early Church (Penguin, 1990)

For a general account of Greek philosophers and their teachings see Frederick Copleston SJ: A History of Philosophy, Vol. 1 (Burnes and Oates, 1975)

Chapter 4: A History of the Soul

Plato, *Phaedo* in 'The Last Days of Socrates' (Penguin Classics)

Desmond C. Dennett: Consciousness Explained (Penguin, 1991)

John Searle: Minds, Brains and Science – 1984 Reith Lectures (BBC, 1984)

See also Susan Greenfield: 'The Private Life of the Brain' (Penguin, 2002)

Chapter 5: Time and Freedom

Augustine of Hippo: A Handbook of Faith, Hope and Love.

For some basic ideas in Quantum Theory see Davies and Betts: Quantum Mechanics (Stanley Thornes, 1999), Chapter 1.

For relativity theory and the concept of imaginary time see Stephen Hawking, A Brief History of Time.

Roger Penrose: The Road to Reality – A complete guide to the laws of the universe (Jonathan Cape, 2004)

Chapter 6: Towards a Natural Theology

It is helpful to look at some of the arguments of David Hume, especially in the 'Dialogues Concerning Natural Religion'. His chapter on miracles in the 'Enquiry' is also very significant.

See also the range of articles in Brian Davies, 'Philosophy of Religion' (Oxford, 2000), pp. 245 – 301.

For radical rejections of theism on scientific grounds see Richard Dawkins, 'The Blind Watchmaker' (Penguin, 1988).

For a physicist's approach to theology, see John Polkinghorne, 'Reason and Reality: the relationship between science and theology' (SPCK, 1991).

Chapter 7: The Problem of Evil

For a presentation of the range of views here, see Stephen T. Davis: Encountering Evil (Edinburgh, 1981).

Chapter 8: Knowing and Believing in God

It may be helpful to look at some of the arguments concerning belief, knowledge and experience in Brian Davies, 'Philosophy of Religion' (Oxford, 2000) pp. 356 – 389

For a radical 'anti-real' use of the philosophy of Wittgenstein in matters of religious experience and activity see Don Cupitt, 'Taking Leave of God' (SCM, 1981)

Chapter 9: Reading the Tradition (1)

There are various approaches to Old Testament history.

For an optimistic approach see John Bright: A History of Israel (SCM, 1989)

For a more sceptical approach see J. Alberto Soggin: An Introduction to the History of Israel and Judah (SCM, 1993)

Chapter 10: Sacraments and the Eucharist

A classic collection of material on the history of the Eucharist is Joseph Jungmann's, 'Mass of the Roman Rite' (translators Brunner and Riepe, London, 1959).

There is plenty of historical material too in 'The Study of Liturgy', Ed. Jones, Wainwright, Yarnold (SPCK, 1983).

Formal statements of the doctrine of transubstantiation are to be found in St. Thomas Aquinas, the Summa Theologiae, and in the documents of the Council of Trent - See N. Tanner SJ (ed.), 'Decrees of the Ecumenical Councils' (London, 1990).

Chapter 11: Sacrifice and Salvation

For an introduction to the ideas of Girard see Michael Kirwan SJ: 'Discovering Girard' (DLT, 2004)

For classical texts:

Augustine of Hippo, 'An Enchiridion of Faith, Hope and Love' [esp. 33, 48 – 52, 108].

Anselm of Canterbury, 'Cur Deus Homo?'

Chapter 12: The Christian Way

The line of enquiry here has been stimulated by the following books:

Plato, 'Gorgias', 'The Republic' – esp chapter 7 - (available in Penguin Classics)

Iris Murdoch, 'The Sovereignty of the Good' (RKP, 1970)

Alasdair MacIntyre, 'After Virtue: A Study in Moral Theory' (Duckworth, 1981).

Sabina Lovibond, 'Realism and imagination in Ethics' (Basil Blackwell, 1983).

John Paul II, 'Veritatis Splendor' (CTS, 1993)

Chapter 13: Reading the Tradition (2)

For a judicious insight into Christianity and paganism before Constantine see Robin Lane Fox, Pagans and Christians (Penguin, 1988)

Chapter 14: Resurrection of the Word

For a comprehensive introduction to the New Testament texts, their background and their history, see Raymond E. Brown, 'An Introduction to the New Testament' (London, 1997).

For a set of insightful essays on the nature and function of scriptural text, see 'Reading Texts, Seeking Wisdom', Ed. David F. Ford and Graham Stanton (London, 2003).

Acknowledgements

Work on this series of essays began in 2002 and since that time a very large number of long suffering friends, family, former pupils and fellow-Jesuits have been subjected to various versions at various stages of development.

I am grateful for the supportive observations from Simon and Jadzia Bruton, Brian and Tricia Pickup and Pete and Bernie Simmons (the team), from the Living Theologians who attended my courses in Durham between 2003 and 2005, and from Joanna Clark, Julia Williams, Gerry Hughes SJ, Michael Barnes SJ, James Hanvey SJ, James Hatt, Martin Pickup, Chris and Cath Marooney and the Merivales amongst many others.

I am very grateful to the Jesuit community at Campion Hall, Oxford for putting me up during my bouts of writing over the last few years and for their moral and practical support. Thanks especially to Philip Endean SJ for the loan of the laptop. Thanks are due to my Provincials, Fr. David Smolira SJ and Fr. Michael Holman SJ for their continuing support in this project.

Finally, many thanks to Fr. Joseph Laishley SJ for his careful criticism of earlier drafts of the text, to Lucy Moffatt for copy-editing this version and to Peter Scally SJ for making an online version of this text available on www.jesuit.org.uk.

3227135R00132

Printed in Great Britain
by Amazon.co.uk, Ltd.,
Marston Gate.